THE EVENING STAR

COLETTE

The Evening Star

Recollections

Translated from the French by
DAVID LE VAY

PETER OWEN · LONDON

ISBN 0 7206 0212 2

Translated from the French
L'Étoile Vesper (Souvenirs)

PETER OWEN LIMITED
12 Kendrick Mews Kendrick Place London SW7

First British Commonwealth edition 1973
© 1946 Editions du Milieu du Monde
English translation © 1973 Peter Owen

Printed in Great Britain by
Bristol Typesetting Co Ltd St Philips Bristol

PREFACE

The Evening Star (L'Étoile Vesper) is an autumnal work; but of late autumn, for Colette was in her seventies and a sequestered invalid in the Palais-Royal when she wrote it. She was incapacitated by an arthritis of the hip following an injury, which progressively immobilized her until she had to spend the greater part of the day and night in her divan-bed, straddled by the 'raft', the bed-table incorporating a desk on which she kept her papers and did her writing.

Situated in the heart of Paris, with its colonnades and formal gardens, shops and apartments, the Palais-Royal is a unique survival. Colette had lived there before, in a dismal subterranean 'tunnel', and longed to move to a higher level; this she did eventually, after a long series of vicissitudes and removals. She was now happily settled with her third husband, Maurice Goudeket, to whom she uniformly refers as her 'best friend'. Hers was a red room — with red wallpaper, a double door covered in red satin, and red coverings for armchair and bed. Everywhere were scattered books and baubles — glass paperweights, boxes of butterflies, shells and ornaments, crystal balls. Her bedside light had a blue paper shade, the *fanal bleu* that was the title of another book of this period. In the summer the bed was pushed into the window embrasure so that she might be 'in the garden'. Tended by her husband and a devoted servant, and absorbed in her new-found tapestry work, she greeted a constant stream of visitors: friends, doctors, black marketeers, reporters, members of the Académie Goncourt, of which she was the first woman member and president.

It would be a mistake to suppose that *The Evening Star* was written solely in the Palais-Royal. Colette was not completely incapacitated until her final years. She could still go for drives, could visit the South of France, most conveniently by aeroplane;

and she finished the book in the summer of 1945 at a house called Mauvannes at Les Salins d'Hyères, in the Var. But most of it was written in Paris, and in circumstances which might be thought both conducive and non-conducive to creative work. Though immobilized and in constant pain — 'An accident and its consequences have settled my fate' — she came to terms with her situation, refusing to take drugs of any kind : 'Aspirin changes the colour of my thoughts. It makes me gloomy. I would rather suffer cheerfully.' And it is her cheerfulness that prevents us from labelling her a stoic. She accepted her dependence on others; she was resigned to being crippled and old; but she decided to be a *gay* old person, to continue to savour the joys of the natural world, to create her own local paradise — bounded by her red walls, her blue lamp, the window with the Paris sky and its evening star. She retained her acute intelligence, her wit and acerbity, and she was never sorry for herself : 'I have always taken immense trouble not to show emotion.'

The book itself is very mellow, with the mellowness of Auden's 'Evening — grave, immense and clear'. It ends with these words : 'From here I can see the end of the road.' Subtitled *Souvenirs*, it is a fascinating collection of reflections, essays and reminiscences. It darts to and fro in time, a diary with the dates disarranged. At one moment Colette tells us of her experiences as a journalist at the turn of the century, at the next she is watching American aeroplanes over Paris towards the end of the Second World War or sharing, from her window, the frenzy of the Liberation. There are portraits of those — mostly women — she had known and loved. The style is honed down. The reader is insidiously drawn into her little enclosure to share her physical limitations, her unfettered imagination. We share her days as a music-hall artiste, her lecture tours, her reflections on graphology or sexual perversion, her visits to clairvoyants, memories of her mother, Sido. She transcended her past work to meet and overcome old age, pain and death. She was still eager to learn and wonder at stars, visitors, her own life. She remained a craftsman with an obsessional urge always to find exactly the right word.

She had not had an easy war. She suffered through others —

6

the indignity of having to receive German visitors, the screams of Jewish women and children being taken away, separately. Her husband was removed to an internment camp at Compiègne and she was without news of him for many weeks; when he did return he lived the life of a hunted man. And yet she could remain observant enough to note how women resented the comradeship their men had found in the camps. She was intensely patriotic; but hers was the patriotism of the small man or woman who could do no more than turn their back on the invader, make a fool of him, maintain an implacable reserve.

Death is rarely mentioned in *The Evening Star*, except obliquely, a reference to an impending engagement. Yet, for all its flashes of gaiety and youth, the work is pervaded by intimations of decline and mortality. Man is the only animal who knows that he is going to die, wrote Camus. Yet one cannot but believe that animals possess a noble melancholy that presages their return to nature; and it is just this sense — in one always so close to the animal creation — that is manifest in *The Evening Star*: 'Nothing perishes, it is I who am drawing away.'

L'Étoile Vesper was first published in Switzerland in 1946. It was offered for sale in very unfavourable circumstances in Paris, without advertisement, on Bastille Day. It is not surprising that no more than 10,000 copies were sold, and that this very moving book has never become as widely known as it deserves.

DAVID LE VAY

THE EVENING STAR

One

'Are you all right?'

'Fine.'

'What's that you're writing?'

'Oh, nothing! I scratch on the paper and then tear it up. When I can't make anything of it, I destroy it!'

Tonight the sky is lowering, a breath of air through the open window heralds the thaw. It is time to close the sun-faded curtains.

My solicitous companion will go on thinking that I am bored. The healthy always believe that forced inactivity gives rise to boredom. It is a great error, into which I should no doubt fall myself, if, instead of having a defective leg, I lacked an arm. An infirmity becomes an affliction during the first year, when every season, every day almost, informs us of a new restriction, demands a new renunciation, the acknowledgment, from ourselves to ourselves, of having shaken today the chain which is to be more firmly riveted tomorrow. The seasons' cycle over, to acknowledge the fetters of the previous year and their mark is already to accept them like a garment rendered tolerable by age. If we are to be shaped by misfortune, it's as well to accept it. We do well to adapt misfortune to our requirements and even to our convenience. This is a mode of exploitation to which the young and robust are ill-suited, and I can well understand the difficulty of making them appreciate, for instance, that near-immobility is a gift. But give me, for a long illness, the child or the old man, who are alike in endurance once they perceive in good faith that what is commonly termed a martyrdom is more easily borne than a thorn under the fingernail or a bad whitlow. . . .

There's been a ring at the door.

'Madame, it's an ugly customer with two wild rabbits stuffed under his shirt. He says they're worth two hundred francs apiece, but he'll let you have one at a hundred and fifty.'

'Why?'

'Because it's Madame.'

But how can this ugly customer know that I am I when I find it so difficult to realize it myself?

'Does Madame wish to see him?'

No. Neither him nor the little wild rabbit with glazed and bluish eye, marked by the cord round its neck. The dogs of Paris may well stop, petrified, at the scent of this man's passage, true savage of the nearby forests, furtive bearer of dangling heads and matted feathers. . . . I won't see the little wild rabbit.

'I'm going out.'

'In this weather! I don't envy you.'

'Are you all right? You're not expecting anyone?'

'No one.'

It is a half-truth. Yet I can hardly admit to my best friend that I'm waiting for the spring. What should I wait for, if not the spring? I am its creditor, this year. It owes me the autumnal renewal which we haven't had, that febrile spasm which re-lights the candles of the chestnut-trees, brings out the lilac in October, and forces unexpected leaves from the bare branches, in fact the crisis we call St Martin's Summer. For no one thinks, twice in the same year, to call what is spring-like, spring.

The feeling of anticipation applies only to the real spring. Before then, and afterwards, we go by the harvest, count on the vintage season, hope for the thaw. One doesn't await the summer, it imposes itself; one dreads the winter. For spring alone we become like the bird beneath the eaves, like the deer when, on a certain night, it breathes in the winter forest the unexpected mist that warmly heralds the approach of the new season. Annually a profound credulity possesses the world, prematurely releasing the song of the birds, the bee's flight. A few hours—and we subside into the common misery of enduring the winter and awaiting the spring. . . .

'It's freezing here! Pauline!'

'Naturally, Madame. It's to be expected, it's not nearly spring yet.'

. . . which never arrives when we expect it. It arrives — we used to say as children—in a carriage, that is, it rides in and irrupts on a chariot of thunder, lashed by great zig-zags of lightning. Another year, before dawn, it lays icy shards everywhere, on the hens' trough, on the filled bucket, even in the footprints of the cattle by the edge of the pond. As soon as the sun touches them they explode in splinters of thin tinkling ice, and the frost, just when we want to imprint our name on it with a fingertip, vanishes like breath on a mirror.

Or else, as on the day of my last marriage, the springtide wipes out in a morning all the good work of an April already well advanced, fills the sky with grey flock which comes down as snow like a burst eiderdown. And yet it wasn't cold, that morning; what velvety snow! It clung to the yellow catkins of the hazel-trees and fell so thickly that I begged my old friend, and new husband, to stop the car so that I might hear the snow whisper on the bed of dead leaves. It is a very gentle, almost articulate, murmur. I've tried to describe it more than once. To compare it to the quiet praying of a crowd at worship is to fail once more, especially if I omit to mention that it is accompanied and accentuated by another rustling, like the diligent turning of silky pages. Beautiful April snow. . . . The wild honeysuckle of Vaux-de-Cernay held it piled on its new little ears, and the water rushing from the springs was like the blue of a snake.

The menu of the wedding breakfast did not belie this wintry passage in the spring. It comprised melting knuckles of pork, cooked in casserole, dressed in their own pink lard and crackling, moistened with their gravy flavoured by a little celery, a little nutmeg, a little horse-radish, and all those wholesome vegetables which devote their aroma to their mistress meat. We had pancakes too. . . . Can one get married without champagne? Yes, if the champagne is made to retreat by one of those chance encounters that used to brighten our French inns, in the shape of an anonymous vintage, dark and golden as a Spanish shrine, which held its own with the pork and the cheese. . . .

'I'm back again. What weather! Are you all right?'
'Fine.'
'I hope you're not working.'
'God forbid! Just the opposite, I'm playing.'
. . . On another occasion the springtide is reminiscent of a submerged rose. It gleams under the water, all gay showers and mosses grown in a few hours. From a green fingernail, at the tip of a branch, a drop drips endlessly, another drop and yet another, feeding the singing subterranean cascades. The seed is moist, the grass is juicy, the bark peels, the sticky clay entraps the foot. But a dull glimmer clings to each ripple of the overflowing water, the iris unsheathes itself in a moment, and the rain is warm. At twilight the river smokes like a rubbish-fire. . . .

A first green film clings to the sides of the trunks that face the north-east. An insidious odour ascends to the ground floor from the cellar. 'What is it that smells so?' What smells so is a full barrel, denatured by this damp mouldy spring, whose wine turns to vinegar. Too late, the cask is delivered of an enormous matrix, a kind of horrible octopus, violet and gelatinous. . . .

A great clamour from the housewives : 'The cider is ruined!' They emerge from the storeroom mourning the cider, brandishing a jug full of a liquid dark and murky as old beer, which has lost all its virtue.

Everything smells sour and acid, like a used-up gherkin, like apple *marc*, like silaged beetroot. . . . It's your smell, you mouldy spring! And yet, if the sun and wind only change their mind, you can still become the fertile muddy road, the sour alley, that leads us to the most beautiful time of the year; there's just time to freeze up this mildew, to serve one last little dish — a passing shower — on the platter-like flower of the laurustinus, and the torrid spring will hurl itself at the blossoms.

It's the most difficult period to evoke. I grasp it by a bud, a wormlike shoot, a viburnum, and pull it cautiously towards me. . . . Silence and heat reign over the bare fields. A varied feeble population crawls, flutters, subsides again. Legs feebly grope and stagger, bellies crawl; everywhere an insect perishes at the brink of life, a milky larva exudes its white blood, the chrysalis bursts like a pod. In the subterranean darkness a massacre is in progress. For every creature so despatched a door was about to open and has not opened. . . . Does the rage to die exceed the rage to be born?

It is the scorching springtime, which stunts the grass and the spears of the wheat. An east wind, no dew, the rosebush drops its unopened buds, the cherry-tree its wrinkled cherries, the young garlic and sensitive shallot swoon away — pity the winged pea-flower which begs for rain to transform it into a pod. . . .

I also superimpose on this strident spring the idea of love, if only to recall the callous selfishness of the loving design, its private barrack-room language — for what modest young girl, besotted by love, doesn't secretly scourge her rival by calling her as ugly as sin and a sick cow? . . . It's strange that this kind of spring remains one of my mysterious recreations as an old woman. . . .

'What are you looking at?'

'The American aeroplanes going over. Fish flying in the deepening night. . . . They enter the rain clouds like a stickleback its fluffy nest. . . .'

For it is always prudent to dissimulate. To admit that one is occupied only with memory is enough to wound the innocent. And how to make my questioner understand that, though I'm over seventy, I miss so much, with such obstinate strength and intolerance, a sky, a countryside, and unbounded and inalienable possession? Let us withdraw then, my dead springtimes and I, behind the inflated foreground of my pretended turbulence, to gain the shelter of my true patience.

'Your leg isn't still bothering you?'

'Not a bit. I'm thinking!'

I'm thinking. That's saying a lot, but it's said with enough comic emphasis to reassure the anxious one. Can one really give the name of thoughts to a promenade, an aimless unplanned contemplation, a sort of virtuosity of memory that I'm not the only one to condemn as vain? I set off, I dash forward along a once familiar path, as fast as I used to pace, I spy the great twisted oak, the poor farm where cider and bread-and-butter used to be generously doled out to me. Here is where the yellow road branches, the creamy white elders, surrounded by bees in such numbers that their threshing-machine hum can be heard at twenty paces. . . . I hear the sobbing of the guinea fowl, the sow grumbling. . . . That's the way I work. . . . Then, suddenly, a mental block, emptiness, annihilation, exactly resembling, or so I feel, what must be the approach to death, the road lost, barred, obliterated. . . . No matter, I shall have enjoyed myself in transit.

I don't always enjoy myself. I may be engaged an entire night in pursuing a fragment of conversation, a name, a word, which are not even helpful to my work. A game, a challenge. Do other wretches, other writers, give chase in the same way? The pursued object leads me unfeelingly on, it is as elusive as game already stalked a dozen times. To catch up with it I find myself singing to it its veiled homonyms, to its vaguely glimpsed rhythm. If it falls asleep, I sleep. My rest makes it careless and I capture it in the morning, innocently drowsing. Wakening before it does, I seize it. . . . I should very much like, for instance, to recapture the name of the traveller who assured me that in Martinique — perhaps it's not Martinique — at about the time of St John's Day — though it may well be some other saint — the ground becomes covered in a single day — more likely in one delirious night — becomes covered with pink flowers. You see that I am not only unsure about the place, the date, the time of day, I don't even know the name of the flowers. What am I saying, flowers? *One* flower, a single flower, a layer, a sheet of flowers, every inch of soil opening as a flower's mouth. . . .

'I asked for that book you were wanting. You won't get it till tomorrow. Were you expecting it today?'

Not at all, best of friends. But I'll let you think so. At this time I make only the most unavoidable appointments. Depending on whether my bed, which follows me like the shell of a snail, is placed at one or other window, faces south or east, I may or may not chance to spy certain stars familiar to a nephew of mine acquainted with the celestial vault. When the stars he has pointed out to me are not apparent from my vantage point I invent them and stick them up where they are not. For one who can barely stir, it's easy to confuse the stern order of the firmament by craning one's neck.

'We don't have any Great Bear here,' remarked one of my neighbours.

She added, in the same pinched tone:

'We're very badly off for fish-shops in the *1st arrondissement*.'

Tiny pointed lights of distant stars, distracted and dispersed by smothering clouds, spacious throbbing of the planet's sidereal rotation. . . . I miss the great planet, Venus of the watery glare. My nephew explains to me why she is so often unavailable to our gaze. But I like to remember only those things about her that please the ignorant. For instance, that she was wont to cheat, in ancient times, those, with eyes raised to her, who did not recognize in the Venus of evening the glittering Lucifer of morning. . . . And that we say: 'Venus is rising,' when she is near setting. . . . With her third name, Vesper, I associate, I link that of my own decline. Once she used to shine on my childhood, seeming to rise from the woods of Moutiers, in the midst of a calm sunset. My father would lift a finger, say, 'Vesper!', and recite some verses. Then he would fix the feeble little telescope on its tripod, and aim it at the stars. . . .

Soon it will be the season for me to sleep outside, that is to set the head of my bed in the embrasure of the open window. From the garden, if it were not closed at night, you could see my bird's nest of hair through the balustrade. It's one of the attractions of this apartment to be able to sleep outdoors. Great drops of rain hurry from the south, the wind flutters and scatters one's papers, a nightbird cries. Everything enters and expands in the open room, everything that the nights lavish on the lighted sky — the waxing moon, the dawn, lightning and stars — save the great planet which invisibly traverses the Paris sky, effaced by the sun and setting almost at the same time as it does. To thrice-named Vesper, acolyte of the sun, I dedicate my own vespers, and read of her celestial adventures.

17

Every eight years Venus displays herself so dazzlingly that she may be seen shining in broad daylight and casts a shadow at night like the moon. The year 1849 is a memorable one. . . . *Dictionnaire Universel*, you go too far, I wish I were able to toy with time as you do. In 1849 you were a young encyclopaedia of twenty-seven years, and you watched as glorious Venus, visible from December to May, stayed while she waned from disc to crescent. Tell me then, hoary Dictionary, tell me how it was that, on the fourth of August 1857, Venus of the evening, Lucifer of the morning, 'attained its maximum size and brilliance, then shot rapidly (*sic*) to the summit of its orbit, then fell back into the rays of the great star and disappeared with it'.

So difficult is it to avoid lyricism when speaking of Venus. Abandoning all moderation, the Great Dictionary goes on to invite its readers on no account to miss the transits and the apogee, at intervals of one hundred and thirteen years and a half. . . . I should very much like to try, but I'm afraid that I shan't succeed.

Could I but return, tonight, to Martinique, could I but view some isle fixed in the thunder of God, on which, from one day to the next, a pink flower, a mushrooming of pink flowers, a catastrophe of pink flowers. . . . Ah! What wouldn't I give. . . .

No. What's the point of this wish, this journey, this extravagant flying carpet? One can't arbitrarily colour the whole or even part of the earth pink. It's true that the miracle lasts only twenty-four hours. But an entire day of rosy life is already too long. The flower that, one day, improbably occupies the entire available surface, which bursts forth without leaves, without buds, in short, without plans, future or morrow — what is it to be compared to if not a blight?

The wild buttercup, the so-called *bouton d'or*, lords it over our ill-tended fields, flows in rivers, stagnates in sheets. . . . The narcissi in April on the Swiss slopes — Oh, how their perfume disturbs sleep, what frenzy they excite! — are no more than an inverted starry sky, on a green firmament. . . . There remains the autumn crocus, the poisonous meadow saffron, which infests the fields with its distinctive mauve. . . . But no vegetable pullulation in our temperate hemisphere is vigorous enough to transform a landscape.

I've also been told of some exuberant blue flower in Australia. . . . Let Australia turn blue. It's bad enough to picture a pink universe. Pink meadow and pink mountain, while the shore is reflected pinkly in the lake. . . . The pink onslaught spares nothing in this . . . call it Martinique or what you will. Enough of this blandness. I could enjoy a pickled herring.

'You look very serious. Did anything bother you while I was out?'

'Not in the least. You can be sure I wouldn't deny myself the pleasure of telling you!'

There you have the manners and banter of the married state. The recluse has a keen desire to scandalize the physically active spouse, free to go out, to walk, to return bringing the news of the town, a flower he's just bought, the illustrated papers with their gasoline odour. . . . With so many heady smells from the outside world the recluse's heart, however conditioned to its lot, swells, covets, suppresses a sigh and preens itself :

'It's a pity you went out. Do you know who just left here? Guess. . . . I've had a delightful time.'

And he triumphs immodestly, eager to elevate his impotence to the rank of a privilege. . . .

No, nothing bothered me. What could happen to bother me, as we say, for we have long substituted the moderate for the tragic word. Bother serves for all purposes. The cash is low in the till? It's a bother. A friend, whom we loved, dies, his death is a bother to us. 'It's a bother that your leg plagues you so. . . .' Our language diminishes the phrase since . . . since the 'bother' of the war — more exactly since a day in December 1941 when rings of the bell and blows on the door informed us that a man, the master of this house, had to get up at six in the morning and leave his bed for the camp at Compiègne. Since then, what that was really a bother could happen to this man and to me? A ring at the bell still afflicts me, to a lesser degree, with nervous shock, a twitch of the mouth and the corner of the eye, of the shoulder raised to the ear. Will one never get over it? Yet many women who suffered the same experience at the same time change so as to obliterate these reflexes. . . . But I . . . I'm too old to get over it. . . .

Twenty years ago, certainly thirty, my resilient physical constitution would have already eliminated the various starts associated with the sound of the bell. Twenty years ago, certainly thirty, I should soon have ceased to interpret in sinister fashion the sound of strange voices, the noise of nailed boots and of the bell, the lighter sound of the steps of the man who goes downstairs, his small suitcase in his hand. . . . Once they had left, he and the twelve hundred of that batch, they immediately became like the nameless dead. Not a word, not a letter, no longer anything to tell us that they were still alive. . . .

The tenacity, the ingenuity of the women to some extent ameliorated their lot. Their basically feminine, conservative role overcame various obstacles. The women I saw at their work were of the very best type. Bloodhounds, virtuosos in rescue work, in the daily domestic miracle. Now and again one would have a good cry, then take up the trail again; for her prisoner's parcel she needed the half-slab of chocolate, sugar, the pair of socks, all the antidotes to thin soup, cold, dysentery, lice.

This is the first time that I've written pages which revive the time whose consequences developed into the perfect and classical nightmare of absence. . . .

'Madame, I'm going to do some errands. If anyone rings, Madame need not bother to open the door. So much the worse, they'll be back soon enough. If anyone kicks at the door it will be the Little Milkman.'

The Little Milkman is three years old. He is a child who has taken a dislike to milk. When he's made up his mind not to drink a drop he climbs up here, carrying his quarter-litre of milk by the handle, and we make an exchange. He has full liberty to kick away at the door. Next year he will be big enough to ring.

Nightmare of absence. . . . What did I have in mind to write on the subject of the nightmare of absence? Certainly nothing very urgent. I can always recapture what I want to say about it since it is, I believe, indelible.

The silence expands around me. When I am alone, my apartment relaxes. It stretches itself and cracks its old joints. In fine dry weather it contracts, retracts, becomes immaterial, the daylight shows under all its doors, between its every hinge and joint. It invites the wind from outside and entrusts my papers to it, they go skimming off to the other end of the room. I shan't unwind my cocoon of bedclothes for their sake. Greedy for air, I am a coward when it comes to cold.

On Saturdays and Sundays the garden is inexplicably deserted until midday. But a child's whistle suffices to breach this quasi-divine peace. At the time of the Occupation we did not find the explosions, gunfire and other rackets disturbing. But we did find execrable certain jolly sounds which marked the visits of the occupying forces to the rue de Chabanais close by. There were also — profound terror, agitation of our hearts — the cries and appeals of a night when the enemy took away the Jewish children of the district and their mothers, separated the Jewish husbands from their wives, and caged the men in one van, the women and children, sorted out, in two other vans. . . . Can I compare my own nightmare of absence to such separations as these? I do not dare, since my own came to an end at the moment when my absent one, set free, staggering on roads glazed with frost, arrived at the station at Compiègne and the train, reached the Métro and the Palais-Royal, and stripped himself to the skin on the second-floor landing so as to abandon, with his clothes, the grosser of the swarming souvenirs he had brought back from Compiègne. As well as being thin, I had never before seen in a man such non-human colouring, the greenish-white of cheeks and forehead, the orange of the edges of the eyelids, the grey of the lips. . . .

This traveller, exhausted by such a short journey, told me that, called to an office at the camp at the same time as two other detainees, one elderly, one very young, he heard, after the brief announcement of liberation, the soft sound of a fall: the two others released had fainted in perfect unison. They had to be dragged out to be given their liberty. The younger one hung on my husband's steps as far as the station and never stopped stammering, the whole way: 'You know, it isn't true. They say that, that we're free, but it's not true. Just you see, once we're at the station they'll pick us up again. . . .'

The silence over the garden recalls, even in winter, that summer morning in 1940 that blessed the avenues of elms, the flowering rose-trees, the lawns blue with their sprinkled dew, the quadrangle of the Palais-Royal soon to be emptied of its peaceful inhabitants by the heat, and above all by the imminence of something other than the dog-days. . . . In the morning shade a man was cleaning out his bird-cages, replenishing the water and seed and squeezing lettuce leaves and segments of fruit between the bars. When certain moments of a fine day become too beautiful, a human being stops his work or his play, reveres whatever is silent or that sings around him, purifies himself unconsciously by contact with that which heaven and earth and the city dispenses to him — unless, forewarned, he mourns them in advance. Perhaps that is how it was with the man busy with his cages, now savouring the solitude and peace of the deserted garden, now motionless, a bundle of millet in his idle hands.

It was then that a civilian entered the garden. He seemed surprised to find there only chattering sparrows, pigeons indulging in their amorous gurgling, a communal dog who was called — is still called — Kiki, and the man with the cages whom he accosted with a quite theatrical ease and courtesy.

'You seem to be very happily occupied, monsieur.'

'It's early, monsieur. The garden attendants are having breakfast. If they caught me washing out my cages outside the arcades, what wouldn't they do to me! But just now I've peace and tranquillity.'

These last words seemed to make an impression on the sociable civilian.

'Peace and tranquillity. . . .' he repeated. 'Monsieur, don't you know that the German armies are in Paris?'

The man with the cages merely gave him a glance over his shoulder.

'I know what you're saying, monsieur. But I don't have to believe it. I shall wait till they reach here to tell me themselves.'

'Monsieur, I've just come from the place de l'Opéra, where the German troops, even as I speak to you. . . .'

'It's true that you're speaking to me, monsieur, but you must allow me to point out to you that I haven't asked you anything.'

The civilian moved away two paces and then, essaying a jest himself:

'No doubt, monsieur, you consider this event devoid of interest?'

'Monsieur, my chief concern, this day as on other days, is to look after my canaries. Remember, my canaries are Saxons, monsieur. . . . Saxons!'

The civilian stopped short, contemplating the beautiful enclosure of stone and verdure, listening to the silence broken less by distant clamour than by the song of the Saxon canaries.

'Are the inhabitants of the Palais-Royal,' he eventually said, 'as serene at this moment as yourself, monsieur?'

'All of them, monsieur,' replied the man with the cages. 'You'd think they were my brothers.'

'To judge from the appearance of the Palais-Royal, your brothers are . . . away?'

'Not at all, monsieur. It's just that they're having a lie-in today.'

The civilian frowned, searched for a biting retort which did not come to hand, and decided to move off. Left alone, the native of the Palais-Royal cast a glance at the carved windows, closed for the most part on apartments left empty by the exodus, and resumed his task. But noticing that the civilian departed slowly and circumspectly, he began to whistle a little tune — a gay little tune, naturally.

Thus it was that, in its urbane, sly, stubborn fashion, the Palais-Royal began its resistance and prepared to sustain it. What

23

'resistance', what war can I speak about other than those I have witnessed? I can hardly any longer leave this window corner in the heart, the very heart, of Paris. It was from there, after all, that I saw Paris sink into suffering, darken with grief and humiliation, but also, each day, increasingly resist. . . .

I enjoy declaring, repeating, that our Palais-Royal, even before the war, was a little province, adorned with a charm and homogeneity that the provinces themselves lack. From a handful of inhabitants the war created a coterie of friends.

Like the other districts of Paris, the Palais-Royal had its *maquis*. It held its hidden parachutists, its Englishmen sheltered in risk and silence, its protected Jews, its children rescued from a stern fate, its defaulters. . . . Did it not also have its black market? And why not? Isn't it a fact that the black marketeer, more discreet at giving than selling, provisioned for many a month a man to whom the German laws denied the right to live, and who never emerged from his suburban hide-out?

To mock, resist, evade, to slacken the torturing bonds, to thwart the spies. . . . The embroideress used to sleep on a narrow mattress in her shop so as to give those who had 'fallen from the sky' the use of a diminutive dwelling on the Left Bank. Quite near me the elegant shadow of a Russian neighbour, thrown on the sand of the garden, would replicate itself at night in singularly masculine outlines. . . . This was the time when, through the arched windows of the *entresol*, the hidden soldiers breathed the night air, the scent of lawns, and smoked seated between the horned shadows of two cats.

Who did not offer his cellar, his house, his bed? A woman who lived in one of the attics suggested to a Jew who was a dear friend of mine — his service record of '14-18 did not save him from the camp at Compiègne — 'If they come to take you away, run to my room, it's not bolted, and go on, hurry, don't be ashamed, snuggle up with me in my bed! You can be sure they won't think of looking for you there!'

This close tacit understanding lasted as long as was necessary. The occupying forces invaded our royal garden only in small numbers, except for rare idle groups to which a civilian would stumblingly announce : 'Here is the cradle of the French Revolution. . . .', except in pairs — a green soldier, a grey mouse — who conversed in gestures on the benches. Entering from the place du Théâtre-Français they shuffled, dragging their heavy boots, in front of the group of little shops and made their exit without delay by the passage du Perron. 'Melancholisch. . . .' The unanimous rejection emanating from every stone, every passer-by, every woman seated by her perambulator, pushed them out. An intense, compact rejection, a rejection that was blind and deaf, and dumb, a refusal to acknowledge the presence of the invader, to read Paul Chack's poster and the other dishonourable announcements, a mental regurgitation opposed to the propaganda waged by the newspapers and the wireless waves. . . . A refusal to smile, to be seduced, to be terrorized. All that offered itself insidiously, or made use of violence, Paris rejected equally. Let us caress with a happy hand its still-open wounds, its upset pillars, its subsided pavements : its wounds apart, it emerges from all this intact.

Two

Fifteen hundred days. A thousand days and then more than five hundred on top of that. As many days and nights as it takes for a child to be born, grow, speak, become an intelligent and ravishing human being; days sufficient for mature blooming creatures to descend, in frightening numbers, into the grave. In fifteen hundred days of war and oppression, of organized destruction, may not a people abandon even hope itself? Our own astonished its tormentors and defied the devilish caprices they thought so humorous.

Humbly, I am one of those who did nothing but wait. Prolonged over four years, waiting found an opportunity to elevate itself a little above a mere passive exercise. If nothing could remove me from here, enable me to sleep elsewhere, banish me from here for twenty-four hours, it was because suffering and happiness were borne better here than anywhere else in the world. Sustained by a hunted companion, then deprived of that same companion when in prison, I took my place in the ranks of the host of women who waited. To wait in Paris was to drink from the spring itself, however bitter. Maybe a born provincial draws on a special faith in Paris, in the light of which it is easier to support the foreign menace, to receive and transmit the imponderables of a beleaguered capital, to adapt oneself to nightly bombardment, to assimilate a war-laden atmosphere, darkened and corrupted by war, to admire the child, to admire the man, the woman of Paris, mocking the crude propaganda posters. . . .

Courage and bravado kept the incorruptible townsfolk going; yet winter followed winter, the dismal summers roasted our arbours from July on. After which it happened that some light dawned in our hearts, some news was heralded in the air. Straining an ear did we not hear an even stifled rumbling propagated

by the quaking earth? No. We were still in the troubled times of
contradictory rumours, clandestine radios, whispered denials. But
Paris was already swarming with hidden men, invisible allies,
with enemies haunted by insomnia who no longer had time to
sleep, while our stripped forests cast their shadow over their
camouflaged trucks. . . .

Then voices, our own, were raised, shouting aloud the names
they had only whispered the day before: Leclerc, Koenig. . . . In
the final hours the great captains lost their names, were called
gloriously *'They'*.

'They' have reached Anthony! . . . *They* have taken the
heights at Châtillon. . . . No, *they* are still fighting. . . . *They* are
repairing the road to let the tanks through. . . . *They* are nearly
here. . . . *They* are here. . . .'

From every window meagre poorly-dyed flags, cut and sewn
in advance in darkness and danger, wave like foliage along the
rue Vivienne. . . . I can't see any farther on account of my leg.
But when the night rose like dawn, a glow towards the east
denoted the Hôtel de Ville, its lights, its crowd, its armies, the
new colour of the soldiers. . . .

How strange it is, how poignant, a street that laughs and sings,
that weeps too! For so long Paris had neither laughed nor cried
publicly, freely. . . .

Gunfire and carillons fly over the dark garden whose windows,
that used to be shuttered each night, are all open together,
pouring light into the quadrangle. Every window sings the
Marseillaise, at every window, wide open, black arms stretch
out against a gold background. . . .

Happy were those, that night, who did not restrain their
frenzy. Happy were those who wept, laughed, cheered, flung up
their arms, embraced strangers, took each other's arm and sang,
marching forward at random, dancing, carrying lights, waving
flags with the tricolour, with stars, with two straight and two
diagonal lines. . . . Happy the unfettered, the children, the
elderly, the curly blondes, hurled at last as if by order into full
celebration, flinging themselves in waves on their rescuers! Happy
those who were beside themselves!

What quiet. . . . If it weren't for the night-bird of a printer who does his printing on the ground floor, the nights would be even quieter, quieter than the days. During the recent time of the nocturnal fusillades, the snipers on the roof wouldn't give up; they ran all round the courtyard and shots were interspersed with warning shouts: 'Don't shoot, it's me! — Shoot, I can see him, he's behind the chimney!' These scalp-hunters were not, alas, from Tarascon. One, who calmly blazed away in the rue Vivienne, and who was caught, had eleven hundred thousand francs on him. . . .

The shots, reverberating from wall to wall in the garden, exploded with dramatic effect. The great difficulty was in keeping back a bit from one's windows. Your inhabitant of the Palais-Royal spends part of his time leaning out of an open window, or at the threshold of his shop. My exhausted traveller, who used to sleep here and there like a chimney-swallow, extracted from me a solemn promise never to lean out to watch the nightly fusillades: 'Those people are dangerous,' he'd tell me. 'Their aim is so bad.'

He would make his way in the evening from attic to attic, in our district or in the Étoile.

For eighteen months he experienced in these places the discomfort of heat, the suffering of cold, quietly enjoying the contrast of the one and the other with his memories of the camp and resisting the friendly overtures made to him by the Palais-Royal.

'Do you know how to climb down a knotted rope?' Mme K . . . the bookseller asked him point-blank. 'If you're forewarned it's easy enough, you tie a knotted rope to your window, you come down in front of the door of my shop which I'll leave ajar, and I've put you out a cushion and a small lamp behind the big Gustave Dorés. . . . But don't let the cat get out.'

Another neighbour, the one who traces with a needle on canvas the blue ribbons and bouquets of roses that are unaffected by war, came with her mouse-like step, with even fewer words, to hand over a key to my nightly evictee.

'It's the one to the back of my shop,' she said. 'You'd better keep it on you all the time, monsieur.'

This was at about the time when Germans — the elegiac sort, amateurs of art and beauty — used to saunter in our garden. One of them, plump and tightly-belted, a Commandant Lust or Lutz, used to try to strike up acquaintance with the shopkeepers in their glass compartments, where trade dreams and dozes, hardly awake even at the hours when the Banque de France is buzzing with people. . . .

'I love,' declared the Commandant Lust or Lutz in good French, 'only three things in the world: birds of paradise, love-stories and *objets d'art*.'

As for love-stories, he bought *Spurs and Riding Crops*, *Flagellation, The Empress of Patent Leather*, and other reputable works.

With a mulishness that she tolerated with difficulty, he insisted on visiting my embroideress of roses and blue ribbons, who also sells antiques. She was barely able to hide her impatient claws behind the most impertinent politeness. As soon as she heard the sound of the footsteps of the lover of art and birds under the empty arcades she would redden with irritation. One day when I was chatting with her she detected the enemy's approach, leapt to her feet, and began working at her door-handle, one of those weighty objects bequeathed to us by successive revolutions that are part boomerang, part truncheon and part axe. I noticed that my embroideress unscrewed it, then returned it, undone, to its place.

The bulky Lust or Lutz darkened the minute shop with his square shape, gave a rigid salute, and inquired about each object. My neighbour, suddenly voluble, took the words from his mouth and the curios from his hands.

'The candlestick? I've just this moment sold it, monsieur, see, I'll remove the label. . . . The little chair? Oh monsieur, it's not genuine, just a bad copy, a connoisseur wouldn't be taken in. I'm sorry, monsieur, the opaline lamp is not for sale, it's been left here for repair. . . .'

She bewildered him like a tomtit attacking a pillaging jay. He gave up, made a heavy about-turn towards the door, and was obliged to open it himself. To which end he grasped the door-handle — one half of which remained in his grip, while the other flew off under the arcade.

The object, in the grasp of a German soldier, became him like a weapon, and standing stuck there in front of my embroideress he seemed to have come to knock her down.

'Oh,' he said in confusion, 'it's broken. . . . I'm sorry.' The tradeswoman was all smiles.

'Yes, monsieur, you've broken it. Don't apologize, monsieur, it's not worth bothering about. No, no, monsieur, we'll get it mended ourselves. . . . We'll have it repaired . . . together with everything else. *Au revoir*, monsieur.'

Right up to the end of the war the angry tomtit's attitude remained the same. And so did that of the other sedentary sparrows of the Palais-Royal. Marvellously imprudent, cheeky, irreverent, insistent on their miserable 'rights', they never forget wisdom and the instinct for duping their conquerors.

During the Occupation this royal palace was a stronghold of pinched adventurous old men, of disrespectful children, of shop-keepers without goods, of derisive adolescent girls, pure Parisian types whom the occupying forces never really understood.

During a sudden silence, thick as a mist, I've just heard fall on a nearby table the petals of a rose which also only waited to be alone before shedding its blossom.

Someone has rung. As Pauline says, they'll be back. Nevertheless, one of these days I'd like to change this electric jingling for a bell, a real one, shaped like a black convolvulus, who would shake her bronze leg within her skirt when her braided cord was pulled.

The air, disturbed by the ring of the bell, has settled down again while I made my way back, by my favourite paths, to the past. It's time — since I've just finished, first a short story, second, a little article, a discreet advertisement for a fountain-pen manu-facturer — it's time to lose myself in the most selfish daydreams, a mental exercise which must do for me till the end of my days (my horoscope threatens me with longevity). This cursed fractured leg, the cause of my arthritis, has spoiled all my plans. Before then, I expected to grow old like the roan mare, elderly, tired and resolute, of which we used to say: 'Come next winter we'll pension her off, she's earned it.' But winter would come and the roan mare was still between the shafts. The winter came to an end; just from the sound of the mare trumpeting shrilly in the stable, we knew that the return of the fine weather would see her once more out on the roads with us, climbing the gradients with stepping gait, stopping to browse with her worn teeth on the new shoots. She did not like to rest.

I shouldn't have needed as much begging as she did to accept my retirement and my grazing, for I have loved — with a most ill-requited love — rest, and even sloth. But I should have stayed longer in harness, retained my taste for the road. An accident and its consequences have settled my fate. I don't complain that it offers me the pleasure of staying put, whereas that of the young and healthy is to go out. My fate demands only resignation — not that it's easy — and harmony between past and present. I have devoted a little time to assimilating the recent past, in the shape of 'war' and 'memories of Compiègne', which I wanted to absorb, then reject and bring up. But the released prisoner gave me no help and answered every question with a disarming patience: 'I've forgotten. . . . It wasn't so bad. . . .'

It may well be that he suffered in another way, once he was back with us. For, barred from ordinary existence, from his pleasures and recreations, banned from entertainments like a punished schoolboy, from restaurants as if he were a leper, from all work as if he were a mental defective, I wonder if he did not prefer the bloodlessness of Compiègne to the eighteen months that followed his 'liberation'. The existence of a Jew, during the Occupation, depended on a kind of insane bureaucracy, complicated by violet symbols imprinted with a rubber stamp, a sign in the shape of a star applied to the left flank, by brutalities worthy of Doctor Goudron and Professor Plume,* by a methodical and always heavily menacing interference. During the last eighteen

* Sadistic characters in a Grand Guignol drama. (Tr.)

months he whom I call my best friend would leave our roof every night to go and sleep, here, there, everywhere, his peaceful sleep of the condemned.

I marvel that I am capable of putting into writing the memories evoked by the ringing of a bell. It's just that one tires of everything, even of keeping silent. I care for nothing of what the war years bequeathed to me. Not even the trying passivity, devoted less to deceiving the occupying forces than to inspiring optimism among the occupied, since optimism is a matter of contagion. Sombre, dark, dissimulating, fuming, presenting a smiling mask, dry-eyed, I yearned, like everyone else, for the return of a time, before the war, that we used to find just bearable before having experienced what was to follow. Among other earthly blessings I longed for the freedom it would grant me to relish my sadness. 'Oh, when everything's all right again I'll let myself go, I'll cry in buckets. . . .' That's what one says at the time.

Three

It is usual to exclude the public from the garden when it snows. The snow is shut in. It becomes free to assume its snowy colours, to know that it is pink when the sun rises, blue along the zones of shadow, coppery beneath the setting sun.

In former years, up to 1943, I used to see, winter and summer, the woman who leaned up against the gate. I've already spoken of this woman, who had imparted to me that supreme confidence, the anguished appeal to another person :

'My name is Renée and I'm from the Cher.'

She owed her charm of manner to an exceptionally healthy appearance, for she was not beautiful. Her well-turned leg projected from her very short skirt. There was no obvious make-up to indicate her profession; the rare promenaders of the Palais-Royal, lovers of twilight and the parallel shadows of the colonnade, seemed to set little store on facial attractions.

During the year 1942, Renée, from the Cher, disappeared. In 1943 a woman propped against the gate made me a furtive gesture and I did not immediately recognize her.

'What, is it you, Madame Renée?'

'Yes,' she said. 'That is, it is and it isn't.'

She changed feet, rested crookedly on one leg : 'I've been in Munich. And at other places as well. *They* picked me up.'

She spoke in a low tone, defiantly turning from side to side her new face of an old woman.

'Yes, in Munich. In a restaurant at first, where *they* made me work as a waitress. But *they* made me carry boiling-hot dishes the whole time, from on the stove, pots with nothing to hold them by. Look at my fingers, they're like clams. I can hardly sew, me who used to sew so beautifully. . . . No, the backs of my hands, that's something else, that's because *they* put me on to winding wool, but there it was women who were in charge of us.

They said I didn't work fast enough and those marks you see there are from their nails. After that I was in prison. . . .'

She changed feet and spoke more quietly.

'It's unbelievable, what went on in prison. They left a young girl for eighteen months without the least ray of light. . . . I must be off, it smells too much of mignonette round here. . . . I'll tell you some other time about my foot, why I limp. . . .'

And limping, she made off rapidly and melted into the distance beneath the quiet geometry of the arcades, extended by the evening to infinity. I never again encountered the passer-by whose country of election was the Palais-Royal, and who clung with both hands to the gate to pour out to me whatever she felt brooked no delay :

'There's never a man comes into my room. For what I have to do with men Paris is big enough.'

She fell silent, then began again :

'I've got a bowl of goldfish in my room. To put under the bowl I've embroidered a round doily in a poppy design. It's really sweet.'

One day she said with pride :

'I've one brother, I brought him up on my own. With the money I made here. I was well rewarded, he married a school-teacher. Of course, she doesn't know I exist.'

On days of snow she would gaze at the garden as if this forbidden white rectangle were the symbol of an inaccessible freedom. I had promised her a book, which would have been fittingly placed in the ruined hands of this daughter of the night. My former books took shape mostly at night, between ten o'clock and three in the morning. This fruitful nocturnal labour — the indulgence of a writer relieved of telephone calls, friendly visits, or anyone's concern — continues with difficulty after the age of sixty. As age advances it's not a bad idea to grant insomnia its rights, but it's risky to hope for it to be productive. Nowadays, I can indulge in reading novels, tales of travel, and that kind of light agreeable study that consists of returning to books one has already read.

Only journalism, ogre that battens on regular rations at fixed

34

hours, constrains to its nightly service the scrag-end of old scribblers. But journalism is a breathless occupation. Even when I was young I was never able to adapt my slow rhythm to the pace of the great dailies.

The obsession with overdue copy, with lines to be delivered between midnight and two in the morning, has for long held the same place in my dreams as the 'examination dream'. It sometimes comes back to me still, alternating with the ineluctable obligation to sing 'Les Huguenots' on the stage of the Opéra. With this difference, that the dream about the article is accompanied by neither pity nor reprieve, whereas at the Opéra I hope to conceal my deficiencies by an articulation drowned by the orchestra and plenty of expression. . . . From the height of the journalistic fantasy there spill several scalding words from the typographical glossary, such as: 'Two o'clock strikes at one fifty-five', and I wake up. . . .

In the middle of the Great War I made my début in dramatic criticism in the *Éclair*, engaged by its editor, René Wertheimer, a scholarly Jew, amicable and paternal. This winter's work seemed hard to me, because it was. The night, the war, the rain, the snow. I put asbestos insoles in my shoes, which thereby became too tight. The last underground train did not wait for me, and I was living in Auteuil. Sometimes Wertheimer, around half past one in the morning, on dress-rehearsal nights, would notice my fatigue and suggest with pretended indifference: 'If you'll give me another three-quarters of an hour, I'll take you on your way, I've got my old rattletrap.' I would wait.

At that time the *Éclair* was housed in one of the old buildings in the centre of Paris. These are so enormous that one can never explore them completely. I recall seeing Wertheimer descend from the attics, where he had discovered a charming pastel, a portrait of a young woman. The oval setting, the rose in the corsage and the blue ribbon in the hair dated from the eighteenth century. O unfathomable, inexhaustible Paris. . . .

The old-style editorial office naturally contained a long green table, a baccarat table of the gloomiest kind. A bomb from a zeppelin that destroyed a building nearby tumbled us all out of our chairs one night, but the house remained standing. Didn't you turn up there once, Francis Carco, so young in your uniform? I can see your tawny bird's-nester's eye. . . . If my stay at the *Éclair* has not left any more striking memories, it's because the war took first place. Its heavy-laden cloud darkens a long train of tortuous months, in which we trace our recollections more and more imperfectly. At every turning-point some error looms up or takes wing, an unintended falsehood, a hoary thirty-year-old truth which shirks the facts and respects appearances.

But as for that which dates from before '14-18 and will never return, what can bring that to mind if not my own especial and well-attuned reflections — and collections of such frivolous old magazines as *Gil Blas*? . . . Who will tell us whether the publication of Liane de Pougy's novel, *L'Insaisissable*, in 1898, caused a stir? The newspapers' society gossip carried news of the demi-monde to the distant provinces, detailed the decor of Mme Liane de Vries: brocaded ceiling, appliqué curtains, period chaises-longues and, on the drawing-room mantelpiece, a clockwork rabbit. Nineteen hundred. . . . the Exhibition? Yes, but above all the list of guests who attended the luncheons given by the Comte de Fels 'in his smart apartment in the avenue Mac-Mahon'. . . .

Suddenly it was no longer a matter of so many pleasures. One no longer read, heard, printed the names of Félisque Faure, of Nini Toutcourt; women no longer had the same names, the same breasts, the same buttocks, the demi-mondaines stopped getting up late, drinking frothy chocolate in bed while toying with a small dog, pouring half a litre of expensive perfume into their baths.

They say that everything comes round again. . . . Yes. Except what we consider as too agreeable, what we regret and blush at regretting. All at once the old frivolous journals contained nothing but men's names and politics. Public opinion became greatly concerned with the editors, proprietors, founders and financiers of newspapers. Some of these were friends of mine. If, for instance, I conjure up Gustave Téry's beaming countenance, founder of *L'Oeuvre*, a violent polemist masked by his plumpness,

36

I see beside him his editor-in-chief, Robert de Jouvenel, blond, brilliant, a hard worker who drove himself in nonchalant fashion and died from overwork. If I forage in my recollections, the burly bulbous-eyed Charles Humbert, bellicose editor of the *Journal* — 'Guns! Munitions!' — the great blustering Charles fades before the strange man who took his place, F-I. Mouton, plump and vague, muttering in the midst of his fair and greying fuzzy hair, who announced trenchant decisions in a hesitant tone. He had built himself a modest domicile somewhere in Paris and managed to get back to his château in the Île-de-France only at the week-ends. I once had occasion to visit his Parisian pied-à-terre, furnished chiefly with a vast lacquered bed of the period of Louis XVI with canopy, hangings and festoons, and by a study of a nude young man in which the painter Sarreluys had carried a love of anatomical detail to a pitch I could not decently express.

The '14-18 war over, the daily papers tended to escape from those buildings where the sombre atmosphere of a provincial lawyer's lingered on under shell-moulded ceilings, in fine salons disfigured by accumulations of papers, divided into offices, cushioned with double doors in imitation leather. Bow windows and low tables, leather armchairs and rubber carpets improved the febrile, ink-spotted obscurity. The newspapers demanded refectories like convents and penitentiaries, bars like liners, office-boys uniformed like huntsmen or cinema ushers, tables topped with bevelled glass like clinics.

They also wanted, as editorial chiefs, 'striking personalities', as they were called. . . . The one the pleiad of great editors-in-chief took most account of, the crack-hand, groomed, polished, trained in fencing and the use of words, was known to me only through conjugal endosmosis.* And that is not the best way to find out. At the same time I took on the job of literary editor at the *Matin*, making my own weekly contribution to *Contes et Nouvelles*. René Maizeroy, from whom I took over, handed down to me, together with his duties, a great quantity of hair-grips, the tell-tale framework of his Mayol toupet, which he had strewn

---

* Colette is referring here to her second husband, Henri de Jouvenel, an editor-in-chief of the *Matin*. (Tr.)

all over his office and which gleamed like little fishes, caught in the strands of the carpet, stuck in the corners of drawers. . . .

It was already the period of decline for a certain type of journalism, which owed its brilliance to star reporters, valiant and stubborn war-horses. Hedeman interviewed abroad crowned heads and statesmen from the height of his old hat and ready-made overcoat. Naudeau was a young man, Helsey was being born. . . . The photographic reporters did without sleep or food; Roger Mathieu and I, storming the train bringing Queen Marie from Rumania, clung to the bars of the royal coach — God, how frightened I was of the track speeding beneath me! — Vallier, of the *Matin*, conducted his little personal inquiry into the Landru affair, leaped over the walls of the Gambais house, passed through keyholes. . . .

'Well, Vallier,' Jouvenel would say, 'what have you discovered?'

'Damn all, sir!'

He rummaged in his pockets; his hair, twisted into ram's horns, danced over his eyes. . . .

'I've discovered nothing, more or less . . . except. . . .'

He prolonged the pleasure, exploring his pockets. . . .

'Out with it, Vallier, out with it!' Jouvenel said.

'Except . . . a . . . tooth. . . .'

And he suddenly brandished, with voice and gesture, a human molar with long yellow roots. . . .

'. . . and a . . . Ah! Here it is! A finger-tip. . . .'

And Vallier would lay his macabre finds on the desk with a mocking air. . . .

'Disgusting! Dung-beetle! Get that out of my sight!'

The dung-beetle would feign bitterness.

'One can't bring back a thigh-bone just like that,' he would say in an injured tone.

He was secretly jealous of the concise phrases of Felix Fénéon, who could splash a news-item with humour in three lines. One day when the chandelier at the Opéra fell into the auditorium — without, incidentally, claiming more than one victim — Vallier announced the news the next day under this headline:

CRASH! THIRTY THOUSAND KILOS ON A CARE-TAKER'S HEAD!

He was censured in high places, for the headline, in large letters, caught the eye. Whereas, for instance, a lower-case typography concealed one of Felix Fénéon's masterpieces; the day when a mountebank, a sword-swallower, was killed with a revolver-shot by a husband he had been deceiving, Fénéon summarized the drama: 'The sword-swallower who couldn't digest bullets'.*

It happened on rare occasions that I would find myself with them at these morning conferences when I had nothing to do, in an ever-thickening cloud of smoke, among men whose characters I can still discern. Hedeman, a genius at reporting police news, who never had the time to buy a warm overcoat. He died somewhere in the Balkans, from an excess of cold. My good friend, Roger Mathieu, died early and untimely. He scorned his body and all prudence even going so far, for over twenty-four hours once, as to sausage himself in an enormous drainpipe of a rolled-up carpet, whence he photographed at arm's length the session of I don't know what secret conference. Fine fellows, ill-paid, decked with the frivolity of gay warriors. . . . Where is Tardieu, of the *Écho de Paris*, with the golden, rather too gilded, beard? He loved those pleasures that morality censures, but did not sacrifice his professional duties to them. His predilection drew him to young and handsome policemen.

'Why, Tardieu?'

'Because, at the same time as I satisfy my personal conception of eroticism, I have, when one of these caryatids yields to me, the anarchical satisfaction — granted, the illusion — of undermining one of the foundations of society. . . .'

Tardieu marked the end of that line of journalists who could be seen at work in cafés. The greatest of these was Mendès, who, amid the tumult of the *Napolitain*, simultaneously dealt with his dramatic criticism, short stories, verses, and his romantic serial, *La Maison de la Vieille*.

Didn't the management of the *Journal* take it into its head to

* A play on words. *Pruneau* can mean either a prune or a bullet. (Tr.)

39

reprimand Mendès for spinning out his lines, the lines being reckoned to his credit without deductions for the blank spaces? Catulle had a ready answer. The next day he afflicted one of his heroes with a mystical crisis, plonked him down under the balcony of his beloved, and had him murmur, from beginning to end ... the litanies of the Virgin:

> Star of the morning,
> Refuge of fisher-folk,
> Ivory tower. . . .

This took up all or most of the five columns of the *feuilleton* and Fernand Xau, founder-editor of the *Journal*, said not another word.

At that period there was no dearth of men who, already elderly, did not hesitate to appear lighthearted. The spectacle of their roguishness was not always cheering. But they, at least, were cheered by it. They were addicts of the pun, and even of mystification. By stages — I should say, in shifts — they grew melancholy. The melancholy and the little light accent of Capus ended up in Feydeau's hypochondria and the black humour of Jules Dépaquit, inseparable from the steps of Montmartre. Everyone cannot be an Adrien Hébrard.

Two editors-in-chief, as well as a third, called permanent editor-in-chief, were none too many for the *Matin*, a powerful newspaper, and ostentatious in its buildings and its external activities such as subscriptions, official contributions and sporting endowments. Anxiety for its popularity did not prevent it, internally, from experiencing bursts of economy, as sudden as they were unnecessary. An invisible hand cut in two the watery green sheets of paper allotted for public use, everywhere suppressed balls of string, ink, and every kind of envelope in the offices. Before long there was an outcry, envelopes and bits of string and blotting-paper made a hesitant reappearance, preparing the ground for the next wave of restrictions. . . .

The fortnightly turnabout had, among other advantages, that

of keeping going a little cat-and-dog war between the two editors-in-chief : Henry de Jouvenel and Stéphane Lauzanne, who since. . . . Between Jean Sapène, 'commercial director of all the *Matin*'s services' and René Schoeller (who was later to control the great Hachette enterprise), who took to quarrelling nearly every day in the most violent manner, so that the smaller fry at the *Matin* used to bet on the outcome of all their set-tos.

Stéphane Lauzanne, learning from Charles Sauerwein — around 1909 — that I was to contribute a weekly story to the *Matin*, laid down his pen :

'If this person joins the *Journal*, I'm leaving straight away.'

'Straight away seems to me very emphatic,' retorted Charles Sauerwein. 'Do you know her?'

Stéphane Lauzanne blushed for the first time in his life.

'I! I know that circus perfomer, that. . . .'

Charles Sauerwein, who was well-disposed towards me, held out his hand to Lauzanne :

'Goodbye, old friend, I say goodbye because Colette's first short story appears tomorrow. . . .'

Doubtless Stéphane Lauzanne took the necessary steps never to run into me. I happened to see him but once, walking quickly, 'behind his forehead' as Sauerwein would say. From the point of view of actual slander, we went little further than to call him '*Et alors*', because of his ready resort to these two words, out of context and out of syntax, in many a paragraph and even at the beginning of his leading articles.

It may seem strange that I had no contact with the little despot who ruled over the *Matin*, I mean M. Maurice Bunau-Varilla. Endowed with great rapidity of movement, he would cross like magic the gap between his car and the entrance to the Maison Rouge, never halting on the broad pavement of the boulevard Poissonière. A sure instinct seems to counsel the great ones of this world to escape the crowd.

As tall as three apples, 'Monsieur Varilla' displayed the robustness of little men, lost neither a hair of his beard nor an inch of his little height, nor the bright red of his complexion. He closely resembled a theatrical columnist — Georges Boyer — similarly

41

bearded, short, despotic, who used to make as much noise during the intervals at rehearsals as a cockchafer trapped behind a window-pane, and whom Louis Schneider called 'the drum-major of the lice'.

Of this man, whose striking name, Varilla, means in Spanish a little stick, I knew only that in aiming at majesty he achieved tyranny, and that he sponsored commercially certain pharmaceutical products. The entire staff of the *Matin* served as his field of experiment. From chief editors to typographers, he flooded the establishment with mycolisine, then synthol, to restrict myself to just two panaceas. Germaine Beaumont, the malicious seraph who insisted on brightening my hours of journalistic bureaucracy with her presence, came to see me one day all damp with one of the two products that a vigilant propaganda showered on the stairs. During an influenza season Henry de Jouvenel once arrived home in a frightfully distraught state, uttered with difficulty: 'Varilla . . . my colisine, half a litre . . .' and fainted. For three days he succumbed to bed and fever. Varilla kept in touch with him by direct wire, each time affirming that only the massive dose had dispelled a crisis which would have proved fatal. Later the proprietor of the *Matin* affirmed that synthol, administered in hair lotion, restored greying hair to its original colour. He practised what he preached, 'thanks to which,' said Jouvenel, who harboured a resentment towards the institutional pharmacopoeia, 'we knew that the original colour of Varilla's hair was a pleasant, lightly salmon-coloured, pink.'

I never recall this period of my life without a golden gleam, without an echo of gentle laughter to endear it to me : the laughter, the fine-spun hair of Germaine Beaumont. To this great writer, so much like a little blonde girl, I owe precious hours and unforgettable days on holiday in Brittany. I see her still, at the precipitous edge of a smuggler's track, leaning over with hand outstretched to pick up a large slate-coloured snake that hissed in her face like a goose. A charming St George, her honey-coloured hair along her cheeks, she found it altogether natural to overcome the dragon with the forked tongue.

Together, we spent more than one September in Britanny,

in the foam of the equinoctial tides, writing, gathering shrimps and mulberries, cutting out for ourselves decent nightgowns in flowered cretonne, bought at the haberdasher's in Saint-Coulomb. Germaine Beaumont sometimes wrote her letters in verse, 'because it's easier', as she used to say. We talked while sewing. I could have listened endlessly to the utterance that brought to a too-small mouth the flower of a clear and ornate spirit, discerningly whimsical, which judged forthrightly and gaily. She is the best memory of my pilgrimage through the great newspapers, during which so many things and persons changed, even the code of masculine beauty. . . . What waistcoats! I can still see Jacques Liouville's in hairy ponyskin, done up at the back. . . . 'Mama,' exclaimed a little girl, 'look at the gentleman whose stomach is showing!' And what cravats! Cravats of rice straw woven with little turquoise designs, shirtfronts in Chantilly on a changing taffeta background, sailor-knotted ties in antelope-skin, in hand-knitted chenille. . . . May I never see God if I lie. A great deal of Anglomania was necessary to cope with these outbursts of individuality.

Still quite distracted by the war, women forgot to point out to the men that a garment which attracts attention is a blameworthy garment. In the corridors of the great newspapers the female element abounded, seemingly devoted to watching and waiting. The freest, the most expert, kept a morning look-out between half past eleven and one o'clock. On the cane chair, on the moleskin of the imitation leather armchair, they awaited the passage of replete ministers, of slovenly parliamentarians, of aloof bankers. Some had their petitions at hand, others, idle and empty-handed, were none the less prepared. . . .

It's difficult now to make the political atmosphere of the *Matin*, at the zenith of its circulation and influence, appear credible. To do so, I should have had to have participated in it by inclination and to have been initially accepted. Was the aversion that politics always aroused in me visible in my face, since in my presence the spiteful warmth of these discussions subsided or even expired? I was shown an indulgence, a kindness, that could not have been bettered for the village idiot. This gave me even greater esteem for 'these gentlemen' and their offhand way of using the telephone: 'Drop in at the paper for a minute, old boy. . . .' 'I'm on my way,' would answer the interlocutor, who was none other than the President du Conseil, the Ministre des 'Affaires', the Excellence of a neighbouring country. . . . At the *Matin* the 'old pal', once more an ordinary mortal, would use the maximum of arrogance in meeting glances, in turning up his otter-skin collar, in not looking at anyone in the lift, but expected neither anonymity nor secrecy.

Personally, I recall with neither pleasure nor profit that busy, echoing, red-painted hall, outside the offices, where the feminine element was not lacking. Patiently, submissively, they camped on the vast lobby staircases, notable for their ostrich 'weepers', their scarves with which to catch hold of the passer-by, their insistent petitioners' perfumes. The experts backed their guess. They could distinguish between the fine fellow in a hurry, the common or garden Deputy, the stockbrokers; they recognized the 'big bugs', laden with riches and financial burdens, the Louis-Louis, the Daniel, both of them Dreyfuses. At the passage of these overwhelming financial powers they kept a straight face and did not stoop to little grimaces.

They could have taught me, those women, that the rich man is not a spendthrift who is always changing motor-cars, an industrialist with large profits. I wend my way — not too precipitately — towards the end of a life devoid of contact with the rich man, but that is not his fault nor mine, it's just that we had little to say to each other. The dealer in gold, wheat, ships, once encountered, could do no better for me than to try to make me believe that he was like other men, the one by purchasing rare books, the other by writing articles and memoirs. A third loved the country, took my advice on planting persimmons, copied a recipe for an iced drink — half champagne, half claret, a large sprig of mint to refresh it all. They came down to my level. . . .

Yet none could alter the picture, worthy of Épinal, that I constructed of the rich man and his boundless riches. I ended by believing, having heard so often from their own lips the words, 'I can't,' 'It's not possible,' 'It's too dear. . . .' that they were exhibiting dissimulation or reticence when in fact they were at grips with such forces as time, distance, hostility, illness. . . .

I should be sorry if the distortion I inflicted on them were entirely obliterated. For if so, what would have become of the sybaritic resemblance of one of them to Balzac's Rigou? I mean by this the subtle and complex man whom masculine friendship and feminine flattery addressed by his first name, Daniel, the only one, in fact, in whom I recognized the attitudes of possession. He excelled in adding to his assets, multiplying possessions of every kind. An ardent appetite attracted Daniel towards succulence, not excluding that of women, from whom he bred a stock of fine children. His hand expertly weighed *objets d'art* and fruits, pictures — which he liked small and famous — stroked a horse's neck. 'Qua-li-ty . . .' he used to say rather greedily, 'qua-li-ty. . . .'

He put precept into practice. Beneath an unprotected shabby body he had fitted a new Rolls-Royce chassis so as to get about smoothly without attracting attention. In cold weather he would don an ample cloak which had nothing to do with fashion and sport, but whose layered vicuna melted in the hand. Wearing a Louis XI hat, pulled down well over the ears, he would leap into his camouflaged Rolls, passing by a miniature pavilion that he sometimes lent us. He would throw us a morose farewell gesture, portraying a Daniel irritated at having to leave his country house, his cup of coffee served in the garden, his antique spit from which chickens hung. . . .

One day when I saw him passing, alone and withdrawn in the corner of his motor-car, I ventured to opine that, instead of going forth to battle on the 'terra incognita' whose extent and mortal conflicts were beyond my imagining, Daniel would have preferred a hundred times to stay at home. . . . 'What do you know about it?' someone said. 'Is Daniel the man to reveal to you where he finds most relaxation?'

Balzac has invented everything, and the Balzacian character I mentioned certainly had fewer secrets than Daniel. Rigou, a peasant avid for secret delights, who insisted on fine hay for his fodder, a well-shaped rose beside his place at table, a warmed, freshly-sheeted bed and, between the sheets, a rosy servant-girl,

45

that Rigou did not know how to smile. Only for Daniel, laden with those burdens of worry and expense under which men succumb, only for Daniel was there reserved the art of appearing lighthearted.

It was on the rough gravel of the 'terra incognita' that he would encounter his redoubtable namesake, he whom his friends of the *Matin* and elsewhere called Louis-Louis, a gentile Christian name as suitable to his bulk as a tulle cravat to a rhinoceros. A striking face, whose extreme and impressive strength of outline were unforgettable. He seemed slow, yet moved with ease and speed, concealed his gaze behind louvred eyelids, his caustic wit beneath an entirely affected hesitation.

I should still be wondering what he found in my company, had I not realized that he enjoyed being criticized. The lion's pleasure in enduring the fly, probably. . . . This likeable friend often came to the *Matin* at the end of the day. Seeing him appear, I knew that, floor by floor, he had visited Maurice Bunau-Varilla, then Henry de Jouvenel. . . . He brought to me, from the editorial offices, a strangely formal manner :

'My dear friend, may I hope to take you to dinner this evening at Maillabuau's?'

I would assure him that his hopes were fulfilled and inquire :

'Is Jouvenel dining with us?'

'No. Varilla's keeping him. Besides, I'm not so keen on dining with such a fine gentleman. He knows I'm taking you out. I've warned him.'

I would be ready in a moment and we'd leave. Sometimes I would linger to rebuke him for his overcoat of ancient date and its marks of antiquity. He'd finger the whitened lapel, the somewhat shiny sleeve, lower his heavy eyelids and answer wittily :

'Don't you see, dear friend, this is not just an overcoat, but a levite, *the* levite. . . .'*

'Well then, buy a new levite !'

He lifted his myopic gaze to tease me. . . .

'There aren't any new levites. A new levite wouldn't be a levite at all.'

* A play on words. *Lévite* = Levite or a frock-coat. (Tr.)

46

More than the dinners — excellent ones — at Maillabuau I enjoyed the lunches taken with Louis-Louis in his office in the rue de la Banque. Encouraged by the proximity of my home he would insist on my joining him at midday. A gloomy office, a small table, on which appeared the good cooking of a Parisian concierge : an omelette and a veal cutlet with a very agreeable Chablis.

'A workman's humble meal,' Louis-Louis would say.

What was I doing there, tête-à-tête with a V.I.P.? I can tell you, I was never bored there. On one occasion I was intrigued by a hundred little drawers, from top to bottom of one wall; they contained grains of wheat. I thought naïvely that day that I was about to 'understand' Louis-Louis, comparing him with a wholesaler dealer in cereals, perfectly capable as well of lifting and loading on his shoulder a hundredweight of grain. I was not deceived for long. He only wanted to question me, just enough to provoke my impatience, and to furnish me with anecdotes in which he played a part that I might criticize. Were they true or false? The point was that they introduced a pseudo-romanticism into our conversation and, for his part, a deceptive and racial humility that were contradicted by the sweeping gesture, the threatening fist, a sombre and superb tone of voice and a turn of phrase that brought a rapid rejoiner. One day, when — for the last time — Gustave Téry invited me to one of these masculine lunches, not unwelcome to either the men or myself, Louis-Louis, beset by political intrigues and a parliamentary candidate, arrived last in a suit that was visibly new and just as visibly dove-pink. I allowed myself, eyeing him up and down, a barely sincere whistle of admiration. . . .

'My dear friend,' replied Louis-Louis forthwith, 'it's suits like this that enable me to convince my voters in the Lozère that they've a unique opportunity to elect a man of fashion.'

He bought a magnificent town house on the Left Bank, one of those great houses where life retreats, provided with gardens of evergreen foliage, shaven lawns to which one no longer knows how to distribute their vital moisture, nimble ivy that refuses to die under any dispensation. Louis-Louis seemed to me, at first, a little embarrassed at such a fine purchase. One of the first visits I paid there took place after dinner. Staircases, flights of steps, terraces, unfinished salons; staircases . . . the plaster was still wet.

'I am going to show you what I like best in this house,' said Louis-Louis.

He threw open a door, brusquely lit up a white room. He sat down on a narrow bed, grasped a plait of hair, which he employed to lift and brandish before us the face of a very young girl, fresh and blooming from sleep.

'My daughter,' he said.

'But Louis,' I protested, 'you'll frighten her!'

'Frighten her? Do you think I have nervous children? They're used to it.'

And, in fact, the long calm eyelids barely lifted over two blue eyes, and the young girl returned to the depths of her dreams. Her father behaved likewise to a brown-haired little lad who complained a little, laughed a lot, asked the time and did not hear the answer.

The heavy confident paw that grasped and flung back these infant heads balanced its weight of paternal pride and despotism. This is how the wild animal behaves, which plays and roughly handles its offspring at will. This image is the best I retain of Louis-Louis, the most familial and the least human.

At the *Matin* a critical and unfailing eye used to observe people and things. Charles Sauerwein, news-editor, was a shrewd man who died too early, and my good friend and adviser. He showed himself severe towards the 'office mice', furtive women whom he would compare to the crêpe-rigged privateers of ceme-teries. Consequential, rather cocky, a little the distinguished prefect of police, he preserved a lighthearted misanthropy which served to protect him from no small danger : those male dinner-parties, the bane of wives, political and private blow-outs, a guzzling freemasonry. . . . The Commission's luncheon, the weekly dinner of the Group, the monthly banquet of the Left of the Vivarais. . . . The choicest vintages used to wash down the

48

murky sauces in the gloomy temples of La Villette or Les Halles; the tall silhouette of Maginot, a bottle of Richebourg under either arm, would climb a crooked little staircase. . . .

I only glimpsed these feasts, no one wanted my presence there. Grave quadragenarians, brisk sexagenarians, how many so-called 'public men' made a dangerous habit of that most French of qualities, *gourmandise*, of their knowledge of local wines, of produce of the soil, of time-honoured recipes? Under low ceilings an inn-keeper would act as accomplice, piously closing the door on their 'private room' as if to conceal them. In fact, they concealed themselves. Plenty, when it comes late in a man's life, remains somewhat furtive. It rejoices but does not honour.

It is a dangerous period that the public man embarks on when he emerges from his initial obscurity. He finds therein the illusion of a general acquiescence. He tends to satisfy, in artless fashion, those schoolboy appetites that linger with him after the age of forty. Should he totter, his country is indignant: 'He had it coming to him, that one!' He had to have everything, like so many of those who were born poor. He had to have that ribbon, that estate, those white cattle on those green fields: 'Just this million, the last . . . just this sinecure . . . this ravishing woman. I've only to stretch out my hand. . . .'

He had not realized that it would be so hard to refuse what is available to the mature man who has inherited from his youth only the sour smell of poverty. He had not foreseen that a loaded table, cigars, the barrel of expensive wine, the dining-car, the raised hats, the petitioners, might be the prime movers of a voluptuous dishonour.

'What d'you think, I'm writing a continuous novel,' Kessel confided between two aeroplane flights.

'Bravo!'

'That is, I mean it to be continuous. It isn't yet. And then, I compress my manuscript more than usual. I disembowel myself, I smother myself . . . I produce surprises for myself. You know what I mean, I make a fool of myself,' he said with his gentle smile.

I cheat to the same end but in a different way, by numbering my pages *bis, ter, quater*. .... An expert and exhausted worker, our lamented Henri Duvernois, used to calculate the length of his manuscripts with unfailing precision.

'Nothing easier, so many times so much makes so much. My good woman,' he'd say to me, 'what are you reckoning up there, muttering to yourself and pencilling in a corner of the page? *I* can work that out for you, by length, by weight, in *europe*, in *didot*, in *grattenèze*. . . .'

Credulous as usual, I believed that the word *grattenèze*, invented by him, belonged to the technical vocabulary of typography. When Duvernois undeceived me, I appropriated the word for the exclusive use of the Cat, who according as to whether she was, or was not, disposed to scratch her divine *'nèze'* against the box hedges clipped *en brosse* thereby qualified as *grattenèze* or *antigrattenèze*. Foolish pleasures are the most enduring; now and then the primeval *grattenèze* reappeared, with his vaguely gothic architecture, spiked with cat's claws.

Our Duvernois, to my astonishment, used to work at a lacquer table as large as a skating-rink, and just as slippery, in the black water of which I thought to see the reflections of pine-trees, birches, a flight of cranes, a frozen shoal of fish.

'How can you work on a lake?' I would ask.

He pursed his reticent prelate's mouth.

'Not too badly at all, my good woman, not too badly. I'm so tired of reality. . . . I find everything that's unreal pleasant, even useful. I've seen Ophelia floating by, as recently as yesterday.'

But from his habit of rubbing the underside of his forearms I understood that the beautiful table made his elbows cold. It's to Henri Duvernois that I owe the restful habit of using blue-coloured paper.

'Give up white paper, my good woman, it rasps the retina. Choose either mauve, pink or sea-green. Leave that rather melancholy yellow to me, blue suits you so well. Ask at Gaubert's, in the rue du Jour, for the tinted imitation Japanese paper they cut for lawyers.'

Although I was not enrolled at the Bar, the blue legal paper stayed with me for a long time, then I lost it.

'I haven't any more,' Gaubert told me. 'I could have it made for you if you were to take a *cuve* — go on, have a *cuve*!' But I resigned myself to another blue when Gaubert told me that a *cuve* meant twenty-five or thirty thousand kilos. . . .

Writers are not, for the most part, very good at securing professional comfort. Carco plants his lamp at his right side, inconveniently casting the shadow of his right arm on the paper, loses patience and blasphemes. Kessel aspires to work in the Midi, in the open air, dazed by the light, stung by the flies, driven away by the mistral, and confronted in his labours by a relentless 'view' of sea, sky and sunset. . . . And in the distance, for a bonus, the Alps. It's pretty presumptuous to measure oneself against a panorama. Quite naked, pierced with stings, Kessel comes out of it with honour.

I was often curious enough to inquire of them in what favoured spot, in what set-up, so-and-so worked, the young and the worn-out, the well-off and the poor. But these are topics which invade an author's privacy. It's bad enough as it is to have to explain the connections between our hygiene and our work. 'Oh, no! Never after meals. . . . No, no, no spirits, I have to be careful of congestion. Mind you, at a certain age. . . .' Would we make more fuss over a disease of the bladder?

I have refrained till now from vilifying congestion. A difficult page, the end of a novel, are often the better for a hotly-spiced meal, an exceptionally well-filled glass. Congestion then becomes synonymous with inspiration. A quickened pulse, a stormy and transient contentment, are profitable to us. Provided we do not delay, provided we hurry from table-cloth to work-bench without sparing a moment for digestion, a fig for prudence. What, we shan't fall nose to page, struck down by the search for an adjective and by plethora! Which of us, nowadays, guzzles and stuffs himself even half-full?

We are what we are: irascible, finical, nice enough at heart so long as we're left undisturbed in the heated disorder appropriate to inspiration, the errant slipper, the old dress, the late hour or even the dawn; we even sacrifice our private discipline to an older and more personal order of things: 'When will Monsieur — or Madame — remove his papers from *my* table so that I can lay *my* cloth?' For we are timid with our servants; it is so rare for us not to lose all their respect from living with them.

From time to time a novelist evades his fate, finds himself exceptionally well-provided with cash. He thinks to find reward and surcease in the temple he raises to himself: reinforced concrete, a balconied Arnaga, an improved manor house. . . . Some calculated collector's pleasure may also be involved. But the newly-rich either ruins himself or becomes discouraged. He will do wisely to fall back on the daily travail of composition, even if it entails amusing himself with modest little distractions.

Someone has rung. I am not so helpless that I cannot, pushing back the bed-table that straddles my divan, go and open the door. But I don't want any visitors. I'm ill today. To be ill is no excuse, no real impediment. Am I to die without having reached the limits of my various capacities? What was the length of my jump, my supreme endurance in swimming? What were my capacities in drinking, eating, making love? I don't know. I wasn't curious about it. I shouldn't have been picked up, exhausted and victorious, on any race-track. Joseph Caillaux used to say that the habit of sniffing the cup and looking at it twice before draining it came to us — it was he who said 'us' — from a sound heritage, and that it helped to make us live longer. He said further that persons 'like ourselves', who manage their affairs without calculation, have a marked distaste for the formula: 'Will you bet that . . . ?', and that they only make wagers in secret, in silence, and sullenly.

But, paradoxically, my 'cousin' — a cousin of the Casimir Périers, themselves cousins of the Jouvenels — cherished and quoted a phrase of Gordon Bennett's which breathed the quintessential spirit of all rivalry: 'The best way to triumph over one's adversary is to survive him.'

To live, to survive. . . . After so many years of war these words possess immense importance. The will to survive is so alive in us women, and the lust for physical victory is so female! When they notice it, our men can't get over seeing us so ferocious. Hardly had he left the camp, restored in health, though still constrained to the nightly hide-out, than my companion was already reincorporating the sentiments we call 'human' but which — and with good reason! — I've never heard called 'feminine'. I belong to that sex which is supposed to be capable of cutting an enemy into pieces, so long as a tiny mouse, passing nearby, does not demoralize its fury. (But what of those, on the contrary, like me, who are not afraid of mice?) It is very probable that ferocity is our accustomed climate. Nevertheless, I am shocked by masculine moderation. Men whom the war has gashed and injured, on whom it has exercised the whims of its arbitrary cruelty, it is we, nevertheless, who astound you, we with our vengeful fires, our murderous laughter, our insatiable malice, our antics — like negresses — around the stake.

One day in 1942 a German came to see me. This was during the period when I was living alone, and in such apprehension! The Berlin journalist had called on the aid and assistance of a French 'colleague' whom I do not name as he is in prison. When I think of this passing Berliner, I think each time of the executioner Laffont, for both of them boasted a passionate love of flowers. My colleague who introduced him left me in no ignorance that the German journalist was 'ruining himself' (*sic*) in fresh flowers. A certain florist of the Victor Hugo *quartier* made no bones of the fact that, every day, fifty thousand francs' worth of orchids went to adorn Laffont's 'salons'. As if to prove that the love of flowers can be tainted by a monster, Gilles de Rais used to kiss and comfort, before the final end, the child whose throat he had just cut, half through, half only, just half to begin with. . . .

As for the German horticulturist, it may be that he transformed into a guilty spectacle the contemplation of a petal, of a fresh floral throat, of a calyx wherein he sought the semblance of a lip, a sex, a wound. . . . I sometimes think of that German, very dark, dressed in black. I have forgotten his face. His overall appearance, in clothes and features, was dark and gloomy. I should not have liked this sombre individual to contemplate a flower in my presence. When it issues from certain beings on whom dishonour lies ill-defined but flagrant, we do not care for admiration to be bestowed on delicate objects and very beautiful children.

It was a postcard — if I may so put it — which rang just now. My mistrust drove me to investigate and to pick it up from under the door of the ante-room. It is all decorated with multicoloured *centavos*, with *correo de sereo* and comes from Guatemala. A postcard rarely fails to reach its goal. This one had been searching it out for two months. For two months its trajectory slowly brought nearer to me its cheerful Guatemalan news, to inform me that 'my brother-in-law's family is adorable', that 'the volcano of Agua is planted like a magnificent image against the pure blue of the sky', that 'the climate is delightful'. I arrive at the essential phrase, which unpremeditatedly holds ajar the double doors of a sentence : 'A hummingbird has come into my room while I'm writing to you. How he glittered, and how I wished I could have shown him to you!' My correspondent need hardly regret anything. Ruby-headed, marvellously green, having quenched its thirst at a flower, not knowing whether it has drunk it dry, the hummingbird has passed my way.

It came from that South America whence I had already garnered that which is dismayed by neither time nor distance, notably the hummingbird too small to be afraid of man, the mother elephant interposing her flank between the javelins and her little one until she fell dying; an inexplicably *sweet* spring of water and a recipe with whose aid Mme Ida Pfeiffer braved every malignant fever, 'even those of Sumatra', drank the waters where poisonous creeper and gigantic snake macerated together, slept under the tropical skies and healed her wounds. It is comforting today to know that the gentle and intrepid traveller completed a world tour on two occasions, alone, took with her neither quinine nor dressings ('my baggage weighs around ten pounds in all'), and railed against the savages only for the sins they committed against decency of vestment.

I give here the recipe for the sizzling fire-water. But I fear that our young girls, with their precociously galvanized palates, may find it a little tame. . . .

'Take half a glass of good strong *eau-de-vie* (brandy), with a small teaspoonful of finely powdered red Cayenne pepper, and six small spoonfuls of white cane sugar. Mix all together until the sugar is properly dissolved and leave to stand for four or five hours. Then one begins to take two teaspoonfuls of this medicine every hour from the time the fever sets in until one has drunk the lot. Before taking the medicine it is necessary to shake it up each time.'

What do *I* think of it? I'm waiting to have the *fevers*. Up to now I have only had the *fever*. I'm also waiting till I possess all at one time cane sugar, good brandy, and Cayenne pepper which shall have lost none of its potency. I accord this last more credit than the spirit. The spirit is an article of faith. But the pepper, the genuine pepper, the lively fire, salutary for the kidneys, trust yourself to it without fear. One glacial spring evening, in Tunis, as I was wandering about with a fever brought on by hail, cold, and the murky water of the port, I encountered a thin man who addressed me by name despite the darkness; I recognized Federico Madrazo, known as Coco, a good painter and better musician. I did not conceal from him my miserable state of health.

'One thing or the other,' he said. 'Either you've caught syphilis by drinking from a dirty glass . . . it's only an hypothesis, dear friend . . . or else what you need is not to go back to your hotel — watch out for the dangerous pale loin of veal *jardinière* — but to dine with me on couscous at some Armenians I know, by virtue of which you will be cured by tomorrow morning.'

I fell in with the latter course and, in an inn as green as a green pimento, green as a glazed jug, two bare brown arms served us with a couscous which would have satisfied eight persons — at least, so I thought before I saw melt away, between the two of us, the granular Fousi-yama, rich in morsels of meat, Malaga

55

grapes, sweet onions, young artichokes. . . . Neither wine nor water on the green table; on our plates the most fiery of peppers, the *sauce forte* which has never inflamed occidental palates. . . . I panted. The fine perspiration released by the honest peppers beaded my face and I begged for a swallow, just one, of cold water. . . . 'Don't make an exhibition of yourself,' said Madrazo severely. 'One doesn't drink when eating couscous.'

He shaped me pellets of breadcrumbs, as one might fatten a fowl, and the fire of the couscous abated. That of the fever also. Madrazo saw me back to my hotel, not before having paid a bill of some eight to ten francs for the two of us. O times, O places. . . . The least colour made me feel I was in the Orient. I bought crudely synthetic perfumes, but the merchant, in carpet-slippers, fez and gandoura, wore on his ear a little bunch of jonquils and jasmine, moist with a spray of water, and he swore to me that the perfume was distilled only from flowers, and I believed him. What don't I owe to my credulity? As they say in my natal province : 'If I believe, the evil is not great, afterwards I can always stop believing.' But first impressions are always pleasing. I've believed in travel for a thousand kilometres of railway line, and I believe in solitude when I shut the door of my room behind me.

Four

What would a stranger who arrived unexpectedly think of me?
But I don't entertain without notice, and not strangers. Today
my workcouch is strewn with photographs . . . which would spoil
my appetite if I were to eat in front of them.

Andre Lecerf, the graphologist, is at present studying the
handwriting of the sexually abnormal: passive homosexuals,
morbid onanists (it was Paul Massin who used to say that 'distinguished onanist' might pass for as flattering as 'numismatist
attached to the Collège de France') and other unassuming mon-
sters, lovers of the shadow, inclined towards assassination or
suicide. One part of this mass of material comes from Germany;
if it is not the most instructive, we may take it to be the most
unhappy, as it deserves. I can only interpret it graphologically,
the text is in a foreign language. But nothing escapes its essence,
and this is very true of writing. The scandalous curve of a letter,
the arabesque as revelatory as a cry, an insane affectation in
crossing the *t*, a spiral, a curve — what imprudence. . . . Which
corresponds to the obsession, the delight, of wearing pink suspenders beneath a navvy's corduroy trousers? Which reveals a
shameful mortification, a geometry of deliberately incised
wounds, kept open daily? An abyss of sadness opens up on
contemplating the photographs of half-naked men burdened —
with an eye to what joys? — with empty female brassières.
Empty. If it were a matter of simulating, by padding, the advantages of the opposite sex, if it were a matter of the strange but
admissible jealousy inspired in a man by the decked torso of
a woman, the

Seins elastiques et légers,
Seins de la belle sans rivale,

the shadow would be less heavy. But no, they are empty, put to another purpose, these twin pockets of satin or tulle, flattened like the flowers in a herbal, flaccid, inexplicable. . . .

In contemplating these little unnatural crimes, I deduce only sadness. How sad it all is, those lacy garments on hairy black thighs, those hairy thickets round a shapeless sex, those pink rococo garters round a pebbly kneecap. . . . And those wretched faces of imitation men, those female figures fit to be thrown away, those abortive essays at forehead, chin and skull. . . .

Their love-life is even sadder. For they have their romance, their aspirations, their disaster. Some have at their disposal, to introduce sensuality or sentiment into their lives, a bare hour of night, a fringe of shadow, a narrow and restricted space. Their field of operations may not transgress that limit, that corner, that alcove, beyond which there is an accusing streetlamp, a lighted road. . . . One more step ruins their illusion, their hope — I won't add their security, for they have found no place for security in their existence.

How many hesitations does their appearance represent? Here is a . . . a . . . yes, a woman. . . . No, for her straw-hat is a man's straw-hat. But a ribbon tied prettily round the crown brings realization. That hair is too long for a woman with short hair, even more so for a man. The ready-made jacket is ordinary, badly cut, the waistcoat not up to much. . . . But beneath the waistcoat a starched shirtfront forms one piece with a collar and tie, the whole device done up at the back with a stud. No linen beneath this, but underclothes in cotton tulle with baby-ribbons in the trimmings; but there's a short pair of male underpants; there are women's suspenders, long enough to hold up a man's stockings; in short, a pell-mell disorder of vestments which assumes a tragic significance, a confusion, a kind of mix-up of the two sexes. . . . My name is Arthur — no, I'm called Emily — Sir, I forbid you to follow me — Madame, may I see you on your way? The series of photographic contradictions concludes with a pitiful nudity, a vain portrayal of hermaphroditism, in its infantile state. . . . Where are you, graceful son-cum-daughter of Aphrodite and Hermes who sleeps at the Louvre, creature perfect in your totality, promised to us in dream? You exist nowhere in reality. Marcel Proust, and Hélène Picard who did not read Marcel Proust, both knew that there is little difference to be seen, initially, between a pretty woman and a beautiful adolescent boy in bed:

> Les cheveux sur les cils, comme une femme au lit,
> Et, le gars, il abuse un peu trop de son style. . . .

Barbette, adorned with as many feathers and attractions as Mistinguett herself, was the supreme example of a playful ambiguity, an exquisite source of demoralization among the masses. None of us was entirely taken in by her. We acknowledged loudly enough the tribute we paid to her deception, and the more innocent among us would say, composedly, that what they applauded, petticoated or otherwise, was the acrobat, the bird, the way she soared. But they lied. I once saw two photographs at one of Barbette's devotees — devotion was permitted by fashion — one radiant in a geyser of plumes, artfully, half-naked — O, that beautiful knee, nonetheless virile! — the other portraying the gymnast reduced to essentials, bare-headed, a little bald, a pair of underpants screening the hidden sex — a severe working get-up, the minimum of extent and weight, the right framework to support the exuberant superstructure. And yet I found the lithe virile appearance, the mysterious statue of Barbette-the-man, more disturbing, more deceptive, than the despairing apotheosis of Barbette-the-woman.

The science of graphology is a bitter one. Lecerf derives his revelations from the depths of horror, by interpreting a little zigzag design, an abortive downstroke, a musketeer's hat capping the capital F's. . . . That stroke like a knot in a whip speaks the same language, stoops to the same avowals, as the hidden pink suspender, as Masoch's torture cord; or as the cascade of ribbons, fond adornment of the 'proud externals', so little external, alas, as to be hardly worth emphasizing. . . .

By an association of ideas it comes back to me that in the Bois de Boulogne, a good twenty-five years ago, spring's exuberance stimulated an eccentric, harmless save in one respect. He used to take in even the keepers in that, according to them, he was dressed 'in the latest style', in a bordered black jacket, black-and-white hound's-tooth trousers and a bowler hat — not to mention the fancy waistcoat in garnet-red velvet, the shirtfront and neck-tie, and the yellow gloves; 'in fact,' as a burly keeper informed me, 'a man of the best circles, up and about at ten-thirty in the morning. . . . He played only inoffensive little tricks and was quick to clear off, the bugger. . . . Once he left a poor lady and her daughter in my lap. . . . The poor lady wanted to lodge a complaint, if you please. . . . It was just as well her little daughter had enough sense for two. . . . "But Mama," she said, "I tell you I didn't see anything!" I got rid of this fine lady by telling her that it was a matter for the Commissariat de Boulogne, that settled her. All the same, as for my man, we ended up on bad terms. I must explain to you that my wife and I had agreed on a little Hou-Hou when I was outside and I wanted her. What d'you think I discovered, ma'am? My man of the world had appropriated my signal and came to shout Hou-Hou outside my lodge! My wife would go outside all unsuspecting or lean out of the window, and this gentleman would take advantage of it to give her an eyeful! Ah, that was the end of things between us!'

'Did you have him arrested?'

'No. But I lost my temper. I told him: "Don't let me catch you around here any more. Go and do that in the Bois de Vincennes!"'

A bibliophile friend called today. He took out of his pocket a small old volume, the binding of which retained a pleasant faded pink colour. He held it a little beyond my reach, half opened it so that I might hear the sound as of new banknotes made by its laid pages, untainted by any chemical washing; he showed me — from a distance — an engraved frontispiece, the gilt of the coat-of-arms still bright on the plates, then put it all back in his pocket. Before leaving he whispered the price of his acquisi-tion — as much, or thereabouts, as a property in Touraine might have cost in the old days. I feel that I did not show myself sufficiently overcome by admiration. The next time. . . .

The next time I'll let him down again. There's no deceiving oneself; I don't see anything in bibliophilia beyond the pleasing feel, the fine page-setting, the impressive style of printing, the odour evocative of cellar or ancient herbal. The next time, my bibliophile friend will once more be unable to resist showing me his find. For him, after all, I am part of his family, though unworthy and only distantly related : I am a writer. He grants me a much-curtailed right of inspection. For my part, if I welcome him somewhat coldly, I acknowledge that he represents the aristocracy of an intrinsically elevated taste. It was therefore wrong of me to mortify him by not being sufficiently welcoming, I who favour the curio devoid of genealogy, if not of mystery, and even old photographs provided they don't reproduce, multi-plied by an inexplicable fashion, the features of Emile Ollivier. . . .*

'Madame, it's those two. Madame knows them, those two who come a long way. . . .'

'But I didn't hear anyone ring.'

'Madame knows well enough that those two don't ring. They knock, or they scratch. . . .'

Let them enter, those two. They bring me their strange odour, their stories as good as hunting anecdotes. I've known them from the beginnings of the black market but they won't give their names. Before the Liberation they were wont to tell me calmly : 'What d'you think, three times on the road the aeroplanes came down over us. Three times we threw ourselves in the ditch with our bellies in the water. . . .'

A sedentary, my ears love to listen to these adventurers, the man and the woman. I once asked them : 'Weren't you fright-ened?' The man said nothing. The woman fixed her intrepid gaze on me and answered : 'Yes.' Her cupidity made a heroine out of her; why not? The black market is an activity that bristles with dangers. While I was thinking : 'Twenty francs the egg. . . .

* A politician, who became *Président du Conseil*. (Tr.)

61

Two hundred francs the rabbit . . . the bitch! . . .' the bitch was including in their cost the water in the ditch, so many kilometres, the burst tyre, the peril that throbbed in the air, then fell from the skies, and answered me *in petto* : 'Twenty francs an egg, that's right. And it'll go higher still, you wait till next time. . . .' I've no grudge against this deadbeat man, this fierce woman. They extort from me, as well as money, a complacent smile. I should like to know more about this black-market pioneer. It's difficult. She confronts me with an incredible unpretentiousness. The time of her departures for remote parts, for dangers, for haggling?

'Oh! Any old time. Three o'clock in the morning. . . .'

'By lorry?'

'Not always, there's times when the lorry's no good.'

'What then? . . .'

'The bike. But sometimes the bikes are spotted, and then again, how much can you carry on a bike? Next to nothing. . . . It's a nuisance, you waste time, the stuff goes bad. . . .'

What gravity, what formality, to judge from these words. . . . The couple, still young, possess the avidity, the dash, the poetry, of pirates. They name neither villages nor accomplices, but they retain an enjoyment for certain aspects of the life they lead. . . .

'We went two days and two nights without food once. . . .' says the man.

'Yes,' says the woman, 'but when we got there. . . .'

I essay a 'Where?' which subsides without echo and my interlocutor skilfully avoids it:

'When we got there, what did they dish us out for a snack! They'd really put on a spread for us. . . . Bread still warm, salt pork, a pot of fresh cream, butter that was still bubbling, coffee of course: and shortbread to soak in it. . . .'

'You're forgetting the chicken broth! . . .'

'So what, and the two hours we slept in a real feather-bed. . . . I don't forget everything. . . .'

The way they exchange a glance, a greedy smile, these two associates manage to push their complicity as far as that of lovers.

What was I saying just now in connection with Emile Ollivier when 'those two' arrived, so impressive in virtue of their bulk, the shadows they cast, their significant smell of crates, of chicken-straw, of mock-camembert? I was complaining about the strange posthumous and photographic popularity of Emile Ollivier, three of whose portraits by Disderi my mother kept for herself. . . . 'Did you know him, Mama?' — 'I? Not at all.' 'Why is he here, then?' — 'I don't know at all.' — 'Then let's throw these post-cards away.' — 'No, no, they're not in your way, are they? Leave them alone. . . .'

No doubt, if I had a good look in my box of photographs, I should find an Emile Ollivier. 'And that one there, who's that?' my daughter would ask me — 'That's Emile Ollivier.' — 'Did you know him? — 'Of course not! How old do you think I am, then?' — 'Then shall we throw it out?' — 'No, no,' I shall cry, stretching out my hand to protect two, ten, fifty yellowed effigies . . . which are linked with my unreasoning fidelity and the memories we never get rid of when they have spent half a century in our shadow. Some drawers, which I'm not very proud of, so far from becoming empty, fill to overflowing; one of mine boasts a massive German knife-cum-dagger, brought back from a nest of German ruins where a charming American soldier plucked it like a daisy. . . . Dignimont has just given me once more an album of cross-stitch tapestries dating from the Second Empire, with — as suggested patterns — a griffon terrier in tears on a tombstone, a ten of hearts, a rosebud seen from in front, from the side, and in three-quarter view. . . .

'I hang on to them because I haven't given them away.'

That occurs to me, from time to time, in connection with the glass marbles at the heart of which there coils the rainbow-coloured serpent, or when I look at a gold bracelet, a clasp, a silk scarf, an illustrated book, which have kept me company for so many years. 'I ought to give it away; someone would derive an entirely new pleasure from it, a genuine pleasure. . . . Oh! No, no, I don't want to, I'll keep it.' Then I think it over and scold myself: 'The reaction of a magpie, a squirrel, a dormouse — the last two, at least, only hoard their winter nourishment —

a miser's response, a constriction of the possessive instinct, diminution of the object possessed. . . .' Shall I invoke art, the great standby? Apart from what may have contributed to the painted colour, a well-loved text, a sonority, a shape, art has scarcely governed my life. It's not nice to have to drive oneself to be generous. A shallow wisdom murmurs in my ear that the glass marbles would be suitable for children, the silk scarf for a young neck, the small jewel would adorn an adolescent breast. Shall I give them away? Let us give them, let us profit from the moment when I still cherish what I want to give away. Let us make this effort, do this favour, come on now, let me give rein to this gesture, let me be torn a little on the thorn of regret. . . . But I soon come to myself and part merely with a fistful of coins, share only my ration of food. . . . Is it so hard, then, to dispense with a coloured marble, the trinket that catches the light, a strand of gold? I have devoted as much time to understanding that my ruthlessness was false as to growing old. If I give away the toys of old age, if I turn and empty the casket, the drawer, I discover that I no longer cling to anything and that all that was necessary to prove this to me was to cast these worthless relics to the wind. That the visible and the tangible exist only so that a blaze of colour, a cool touch, a style, should delude me as to their actual presence and efficacity, whereas they are really a spasm of appetites that are already defunct.

The attempts I make suffice to edify me. Already I have given as presents the coloured sphere, the little jewel, even the book. And I have waited, in vain, to suffer for it. Did I then love them so little, so poorly? Maybe. Then I must be prudent, that is niggardly, with what I used to dote on. I continue, without further and better inquiry: 'Oh, no! I shan't give it away, I'll keep it. . . .'

I'd kept Sido's blue dress till now, her little short bodice, all gathered and drawn together by pleats at the back, under the breasts, beneath the arms. . . . Only the skirt bloomed widely, embroidered with white chain-stitch garlands. Oh, no! I don't want to give it away, I'll keep it. . . . And it will do to cover the binding of the manuscript of *Sido*. That's certainly a graceful

Colette in music-hall.

Colette receiving a visitor in her **Palais-Royal** apartment after the war. Her third husband, Maurice Goudeket, is standing behind her.

thought. In that way the blue dress will still clothe Sido. In that way the manuscript, on imitation Japanese vellum in three different blues, is well protected, bound by the hand of an old binder, masterly. That is very good. A little too good. It is art. It goes beyond piety, the cosy jumble of crumpled souvenirs : I am no longer so sure that I'm still fond of it. But my best friend, a bibliophile and amateur of fine bindings, is so pleased. . . . One must give, decidedly, and give all. Misia even gave a rival the husband she loved. A test which is not unique. A good many of us have tried it, profiting from a troubled, quasi-fatal moment when the rival touches her apogee of innocence, of beauty, of unreason, and begs us to yield in her favour. That is all that is needed for us to carry out what we call 'a beautiful gesture of renunciation', which won't afford us the least pity or shadow of consideration.

Or else we must hang on to everything and restrain our fine impulses, which risk sharing out our stray possessions. . . . All that becomes remote and absurd. . . . Yes, one must keep everything, that's the truth. But I allowed the departure for the long unalterable sleep of that old sylph with wings matted by rain, my brother, without his having handed over to me what he alone held, our ancient possessions, our ritual songs, the topography of our natal village, the names of the departed commended in the sermon every Sunday : 'The Church commends to your prayers the souls of Edouard de Lacour, Clémence de Lacour, Pauline Beauchêne and Fernand Bourgneuf; of Claude Brunet, Geneviève Gonnot, Toussaint Gounot, Irène and Octavie de Vathaire, Jacques Corneau, Marguerite Danjean, Adolphe Gressien, Laure Desleau, the widow Mallet, Prix Thillière, Paul Gentil, Estelle Reboulleau, Jean-Baptiste Glaumot. . . .' After Jean-Baptiste Glaumot I see no more than a misty file of humble dead. An insubstantial patrimony of words, of images, was lost with this amazing brother, who hoarded only time past. Our few treasures lay undistributed in the old sylph's room, on the sixth floor. A white wooden wardrobe and the cast-iron wash-basin defined the exact and severe condition of our past. . . .

The remainder, more tangible and doubtless less precious, was frequently stolen from me. I have been robbed of books, letters, small pictures in their frames, the excommunications, in red ink, that Erik Satie scattered as a rosebush does its flowers. That's what comes of not believing in locks, nothing of mine is shut away. Where is the little light gold dollar which we cherished like a pastille, the bracelet of chestnut hair, finely plaited, cool, exactly the temperature of a snake? Where has that string of branched, bristling, red coral faded away, which resembled I don't know what choleric crustacean? I search. Foot- and finger-prints are by now effaced. One should keep a watch on every-thing, or else burn everything. . . .

I know of women who say: 'Oh, me, I keep everything. I can't remember ever having destroyed a paper.' What frightful archives. . . . One of these, a literary woman, and charming, reproaches me gently — there are gentle literary women — for always having maintained silence about the 'major encounters' of my life, all — she says — that one feels 'throbbing behind a curtain spread by your own hands, the great experiences that have been landmarks on your way. . .' But who thinks them so great? Close, dear friend, the credits you so generously open for me; I am, from poverty, a bad payer. And then, my dear, I did once try to elevate my memoirs to the plane of complete con-fidence. . . . In a large account-book, devoid of any accounts, ruled in blue with vertical lines, in red with vertical columns, what emerged deserved instant obliteration, smelled of gossip, of botching. So I confined myself, thenceforward, to more or less amorous histories. . . . 'One tells of a lover and is silent about the rest.'

Let's keep everything, out of respect for the ways employed by dispersal and return. A little frame in flecked yellow thuja wood hangs on my wall, and I don't think it will budge from there as long as I live. It desperately threw itself in my path in order to meet up with me again. This dates from the time when I was a regular visitor at the Sunday market, the so-called Flea Market. Nearly every Sunday I scoured the fortifications of Saint-Ouen, their terraces, their culs-de-sac, their banks of worn grass. The tricksters there required no stocks other than three half walnut-shells and a jet bead — 'Where is it then, that little black bead?' — the smoking basins of oil, standing on three-legged stoves, crisped the garfish and the slice of bacon — 'bacon five sous, real bacon!' *Objets d'art* and kitchen utensils succeeded each other in a strange and seasonal fashion. One month there would be an abundance of glove-stretchers and sugar-tongs, which gave way to walking-sticks with knobs of ivory and silver, precious canes with tassels of plaited leather. The following month a funereal abundance of second-hand top-hats was rife. Then there were fine sheets of hemstitched Friesian linen, altar-cloths, damask curtains which had retained their youth in the chill shade of a Second-Empire salon. . . .

Coveting a set of fine sheets, knocked down to Germaine Beaumont at ten francs the pair, I praised the attractions and advantages of the Flea Market so highly that one fine Sunday Charlotte Lyses insisted on accompanying me. She was bored there and made me give short shrift to the rickety furniture, the knives without handles, the handles without knives and aphonic phonographs. In the time it took her to acquire a little chain in smoked crystals I exchanged a greeting with le Barbu — I did not know what his other name might be — seated on the ground among his luxury articles on a sheet of oilcloth.

'And now, quick, the Métro, I've seen enough,' declared Lyses. 'Are you coming, Colette? Colette, what is it you're looking at?'

To tell the truth, I wasn't looking at anything. I had just fallen into one of those mental states which confound the past and the present, the false and the real, where we wait passively to regain control of them and of ourselves.

'You've got a lorgnette, Lyses, would you mind trying to read what's written — it's nearly worn away — on the back of that little thuja frame there?'

'Does it interest you? I can see, that is, I can only just see. . . . I see "Adèle, Sophie Landay, or Landoy, née Châtenay!" . . . . and something else. . . . "Châtenay . . . children, never forget. . . ." The ink is so pale. . . .'

But I didn't need any more help :

' "My children," I recited, "never forget your worthy and virtuous mother." It is signed Eugène Landoy. The miniature painter was named Foulard; his signature is on the left of the miniature with the date 1830. The ivory layer is split from top to bottom, a crack as fine as a hair. . . .'

It was the portrait of my maternal grandmother, Mme Eugène Landoy, née Sophie Châtenay. A portrait stolen from me, gone astray for thirty years, for thirty years struggling towards me, by what paths on earth or beneath it. . . . Le Barbu, responsive to the strange family setting, asked me only fifty francs. 'It's like a play,' was his comment. A connoisseur, Charlotte Lyses shared his opinion.

The miniature represents a young woman with a trilobed coiffure — a large bun on top, a bunch of curls, like chipolatas, on either temple. She smiles, well content — to my mind — to have regained the corner of my mantelpiece. She died young, and deceived twenty times by her husband; all I know about her is her premature death and her silence as a betrayed wife — the essentials, in fact. All that is very far away. . . .

What interests me is the last journey of this painted lady. The thieving hand, the abduction, the halting-places, the obscure places, other unscrupulous hands, the interminable waiting until, perhaps, she despaired. . . . I love to see her at peace in my home. No doubt, before having betrayed her twenty times, her husband, a shade 'coloured', had been seduced by the pallor of that Parisienne of the boulevard Bonne-Nouvelle. . . .

Five

'*Have they been looking after you? You haven't been bored today?*'

My best friend, how can you think that I might have been bored? Why, the sky alone is distraction enough. I'm always aware of those cardinal points whence the clouds flow that resemble Victor Hugo and Henri Rochefort, the wind that settles the rain, the sun that burns the double curtain, the hail so harsh to the rose-bushes. The moon enters my room at will, advances at a cat's pace, extends a white paw to attack my bed: she is satisfied with waking me, she at once loses heart and climbs down again. At the time when she is at the full I rediscover her at dawn, all pale and bare, straying in a chill region of the sky. Returning to its slumbers, the last bat slashes her with a zig-zag stroke.

At the day's end my youngest neighbours have a charming way of feeding my more or less stagnant curiosity. They haul up here their finest products, a pair of nine-month-old twins, fresh and downy as two peaches from the same branch; a little boy, thoughtful and distinguished, who, at three, plays with the most difficult words, such as: stalactites, ornithorhyncus, trochilidae (I teach him them so that he may astound his father); the Little Milkman comes to sing me his latest song and to introduce his fifteen-month-old sister called La Carrée, since she is such a fine girl that she bursts in her skin like a well-stuffed sack of coffee; Anatole, Mme Laure's parrot, leaves his home in the *entresol* — formerly my *entresol* — grants me a few minutes of his frigid courtesy, his judicial gaze and his relentless resemblance to Offenbach.

Sometimes, at night, it's the unknown man who sets out to divert me, calling me to the telephone. It is two or four o'clock in the morning. . . . He asks if it is I, really I, and I assure him it is. Then he says: 'I shit on you,' and hangs up again — too soon, for I should like to question him about his mysterious ailment, the motives for his insomnia, to discover whether, having nocturnally shat on me, he can fall back on his bed to sleep there, at last happy and released. As it happens, he is discreet, only wakes me at long intervals, and utters only that, shall I say, essential word.

There are so many of them, those who stay awake despite themselves. Last year, for a long time, the foul-mouthed Unknown tormented a young girl. He would ring her up but did not speak to her. He breathed a long gasping breath in her ear, a sort of great wild beast's panting, a hateful 'haaahh' which made the little fool very frightened. She decked out this punctual summons with pompous names. She detected in it an infernal sigh, an implacable obsessional will. For it takes little to banish reality and probability from a young girl's life.

I have had other nocturnal callers. For the timid human creature needs to 'say something to someone', even if in the coarsest terms. A man's voice sometimes asks me to listen to a serenade which begins as follows:

> *Poil au bec de gaz*
> *Mon cul sur la commode,*
> *Poil au chandelier,*
> *Mon cul sur l'escalier. . . .*

I admit that these words are of doubtful merit, and that they attribute an improbable hairiness to items of furniture. But what a fine baritone voice!

None of this is very serious. No nocturnal episode has seriously disturbed my nights since the ring at the bell, the hobnailed boots, since the coarse whispering voices, since . . . well, since.

When the stubborn will to live and to manifest ourselves one to the other, the absent one and myself, began to stab sharply, like needle-pricks, at the obscurity of the camp, the massive obstacle which separated us, there was at first a piece of squared paper torn from a notebook, hardly bigger than a Métro ticket, covered with a writing unused to being so minute and cramped. I thought of the greasy paper which used to line Vautrin's wig, of the few lines destined to save Lucien de Rubempré. I thought of all those curtailed messages, compelled to choose only between words of encouragement and words of menace; I thought of Gordon Pym when he deciphered a fragment of a letter where there gleamed the terrible words: '. . . blood. Stay hidden. Your life depends on it.'

I have preserved these lines, the first to arrive from the camp at Compiègne, which stood for communication, life, the return of hope. I also keep a list, which reached me later on. No doubt it was compiled in one of those moments when the name and the savour of the foodstuffs mentioned arouse some delirium in famished prisoners. A list, a litany rather, which demanded, if I could entrust them to a safe channel — thank you, Dr Breitmann! — butter, jam, sugar, and, above all, like a burning refrain, above all 'bread, in the name of Heaven, bread!' And I could not restrain an agonized smile on seeing that the word bacon, the not-to-be-found BACON, was written in capital letters. . . .

They also begged, those who were there, for the help of alcohol, dreamed of condiments and seasoning before and after the solitary soup, barely disturbed by vegetables, between two infusions tasting of boiled hay. Questions and answers, separated by long silences, confiscated, gone astray, did not make a dialogue. Uncertainty still reigned over those first batches, those massive round-ups, and the jailers themselves seemed inexperienced. No routine, no procedure for ordering the brutalities, to endow them with the character they assumed later of a prescriptive ferocity, an organized anti-Semitism.

But the thermometer, after the 1st January 1942, began to fall. Eight — ten — twelve degrees below zero; — fourteen on the chill plain of Compiègne. And the word 'deportation' took a larger and larger place in the forecasts and the news; and there were many of us women who stood aghast, to learn that what had seemed to us the worst was about to become worse still.

Inability to help a loved one is the bitterest of disappointments. We savoured it, ate it, drank it. It left its mark everywhere, made us vindictive, unjust. A little gilded horse, in Capo di Monte porcelain, still suffers at times for my past misery. He it is, his burnished gold rump that the first light drew out of shadow, and even in the shadow he bore the weight of my unrelenting gaze. Today he asks me to be reasonable for a moment, to reaccord him, exorcized, his essence as a very nice little horse on whose gold dwells the first ray of sunlight, the last of moonlight. We were alone, he and I, in the masterless house, and from my bed I gathered, from his bright golden cruppers, an impossible hypnosis. . . .

Six

Il ne vous atteint pas, l'affreux cri des sirènes,
Dans les bars de cristal, éclatants perroquets,
Frivoles favoris des sombres capitaines.

Now she is dead, she who scattered verses like these with a grand air of display and indifference. Running, she would abandon them if one of the blue parakeets called out, if the sparrow tapped with his beak on the window, if the bar of chocolate was cooking too quickly. I find it unbelievable that she is dead and it will take me a long time to grasp it. I cannot even confront such a vivid friend with a still image, were it even that of her peaceful sleep.

A life as pure as hers cannot fail to appear mysterious. It isn't easy to read within the crystal sphere. Chastity, pride, poverty — she lived on these three heights. She spent her last years on the fourth floor, where she lived in the rue d'Alleray, solitary for some quarter of a century. A neighbour, a child, an obliging tradesman carried the essentials up to her eyrie, well-orientated, furnished entirely with leftovers, light furniture, blue opalines, pious images, Second-Empire night-lights, many blue trinkets.

Hélène Picard's last journeys were only from the rue d'Alleray to the St Antoine Hospital, then from the rue d'Alleray to the pretty Château du Val, near Saint-Germain, a pleasant family convalescent home run by the Légion d'Honneur. The trips she made to be with me in the summer I don't count as journeys, although she never engaged in them without agitation, without losing a suitcase, bringing something useless, forgetting the indispensable, enjoying some contretemps, distressed at having to leave Paris just when the Foire aux Puces of the Fourteenth of July enlivens the square des Arts-et-Métiers. Once settled deep in the country, she would take root there with a unique strength and eagerness. Her poesy gained from everything, ennobled everything. That is the privilege of those who are born to sing. . . .

Her parakeets were also blue. When, at the beginning of the war, millet and canary-seed became scarce, Hélène put the blue birds out of her heart and gave them to an enthusiast who was better able to supply them with seed. . . . If I had to reckon up her renouncements, carried out with a nun's lightness of heart, I should be bound to forget some. Plagued by a serious bone disease — shortly before my own arthritis set in, never to leave me again — Hélène Picard also renounced the visits we used to exchange so happily, our conversations in the blue room where this ascetic gourmande filtered her coffee as no one else could, cooked — like no one else — a little stew of pork that was our *plat de résistance*. I would bring the millefeuilles she liked, and creamy éclairs from Flammang's.

It was hardly a matter of number or rhythm or even literature in our intimate conversation. Our correspondence was marked by less reserve. Hélène, endowed with an aptitude for keen and faithful criticism, enthused for or against a new work, judged it with an angelic severity. Traces of poetic abundance were scattered around her. Often one of her mornings would suffice to strew the blue room. The morning light would ripen a poem for this daughter of sunny Ariège, who went early to bed and woke with the parakeets. She rose at dawn, percolated her coffee, wielded the broom, abandoned furniture-cleaning for strophes, and her adventurous writing impatiently laid its spiky antennae on little bits of paper, on the back of the gas bill and the dairy account. With what arabesques, what rhymes, she would illustrate a catalogue of electrical appliances which came to the poet's hand at the tumultuous moment when a poem insists on being born. . . .

'Have you been working, Hélène?'

'Splendidly! But I've mislaid what I wrote. It's not important!'

What fine disdain, what pride, what modesty. . . . She would use a barely dry poem to wrap up the slice of cake, the triangle of mountain cheese, harder than a roof-tile, that she slipped into my bag.

'I hope you've kept a copy of it.'

She would pirouette on her little feet, agile and dancing. She laughed in mock heroism :

'No! I can make some more!'

And I would admire this rich undisciplined woman with the wonder of a thrifty prosodist.

When she did not have the time to write to me she would send a packet containing a bouquet of her latest verses. One December 31st I received *Songe*, with these words : 'Happy New Year and all my love, Hélène.' We never delayed writing to each other for long. At times her letters consisted of pages on a sharply critical note, at times of spontaneous messages, reports that might have emanated from a schoolgirl of genius, sealed with a charming domestic humility : 'Today I'm quite taken up with laundering my big embroidered muslin curtains, the ones that bathe my little drawing-room in a calm snowy light. . . . My jam has come out splendidly. As much strawberry as cherry, then a little more of greengage later on, I can reckon on sixty pots for my ant-like meals. . . . I can look forward to a fine winter's gormandizing. . . .'

I can no longer recall the year our friendship began. I remember that Hélène Picard, separated from her husband — a former sub-prefect, himself something of a poet — arrived in Paris, there to enjoy her poverty and independence; she took the same fierce pleasure in the one as in the other. Still young, very pretty, pale and dark like a daughter of the Midi, eyes sparkling, her chief beauty derived from her proud, fine, sensitive nose.

The enlargement of a snapshot by Henri Laval is a magnificent portrait of Hélène at around the age of fifty. A perfect nose, a sturdy warrior's neck, hair in a devil's tangle, the corner of the mouth parallel to the angle of the eye. What a good likeness, how ironical, assured, impressive! The first time that she came into my office at the *Matin*, Hélène was adorned — following her rather gipsy tastes which Paris never completely tamed — with little pearled combs, cabochon necklaces, écru lace, and her long hair covered her ears with shell-like curls. The sacrifice of her hair soon after cost her some misgivings, regrets, tears even; but she thereby acquired a charming bohemian air, an abundant foliage of curls. Sprightly, frugal, spontaneous, embodying in all her actions the pleasant manners, kindliness and meticulousness of provincial France, it was not difficult to believe her when she assured us that a slender monthly allowance was wealth enough for her. To convince me, she would itemize her budget, counting on her fingers. The attractiveness that goes with childlike women did not desert her in maturity.

She would bolt her door to embark on the washing and ironing of an exemplary housewife and forget, at night, the key left outside. These gay confident caprices, the love of idling and laughter, were only temporary, gave way to a fundamental unsociability. If the bell rang, Hélène would approach the door silently — the door that a blow with one's fist would have driven in — and listen: 'Who rang?' she would cry. Then she might add: 'Madame Picard is not in,' careless that her meridional *a*'s, clear and short, gave her the lie. . . .

Our friendship once established, Hélène Picard used to join our little colony which the dog-days exiled to the Breton coast, and which included Francis Carco and his first wife, the Leopold Marchands, Germaine Beaumont, and two or three children of Henri de Jouvenel's of different beds. . . . To all of them I was most grateful for being far younger than myself, for loving the sea, bathing, silence, gaiety. . . . Hélène Picard seemed the youngest, intoxicated by the sea she knew so little. She leaped about in the waves like a child having a dip, turned pale, her teeth chattered, she would cover her girlish bosom with her hands as with a shell, and take shelter on the warm sand or in a dell of dry close-cropped thyme.

Carco sometimes teased her rather cruelly. But she bore his attacks with a sort of gratitude. Léopold Marchand would invent stories of pirates for her which she listened to, quite taken in. Germaine Beaumont, from her vantage point as a twenty-five-year-old, showered her with so-called practical advice. We allowed ourselves, in our contact with Hélène, a familiarity that she did not attempt to restrain.

But one of these shameless individuals might pick up a stray page of manuscript, striped with verses, read, stop laughing, gaze incredulously at our 'little Hélène', busy with marbles or a medicine-ball too heavy for her delicate wrists; the page would pass from hand to hand and its passage would give rise to admiration, respect, the silent promise to treat 'our Hélène' as she deserved. . . . Not for anything in the world would she tolerate these signs of our reverence for long. But she could not prevent us from being haunted by a verse from her lasting light:

Houleuse fille blanche offerte aux matelots!

Leopold Marchand would declaim on the beach, bare feet in the foam. . . .

. . . Que ne puis-je suspendre
Mon coeur, comme une merle, au cou du rossignol!

would sigh Germaine Beaumont.

How can I separate from those Breton summers the memory of certain of Hélène Picard's verses, fed by an unformulated sensuality, a secret incandescence which the poet did not deign to explain. . . . The Brittany that I lost, the fragment of Armorica that melted away in my imprudent hands, is at least preserved for me in Hélène's verses!

Domaine forestier, ensoleillé d'automne,
Arbres, secrètement sur la mer entr'ouverts . . . . .
. . . .
Le sol sentait le fruit, l'eau morte, la Bretagne,
L'herbe amère . . .
. . . .
Le chevrefeuille errait dans l'ombre incriminée . . .

She gave us matter for thought in stranger lyricisms. The last collection Hélène Picard published she entitled *Pour un Mauvais Garçon*. The seventy poems contained in the volume have the style of voluptuous riddles. Their dazzle, their plastic richness, as much as their gilded shadows, seem to veil a name, to mask an individual. . . . What mystic might not apply himself to discern therein the signs of a phenomenon of possession? This volume, wholly seized with mystery, seems under a spell, illuminated by second sight, thrown, like a malefic flower, at some young, accursed face of flesh. In it Baudelaire, barely astonished, encounters the heroes of Carco's novels, and sometimes their tangy vocabulary. . . .

As for the readers of *Pour un Mauvais Garçon*, I know some who remained dazzled and uncertain, who could come to no conclusion regarding the most singular avatar that an unbridled yet chaste poetry could authorize. To avoid the temptation of tarnishing the poet's purity among so many hovels, pistols, absinthes, furnished rooms and yellow eiderdowns, whistle blasts and bluish blades, it is only necessary to read, or re-read, in *Sabbat*, the contempt held by Hélène Picard all her life for the avid kind of female consumer whom she calls 'Madame how often'.

Printed in an edition of seven hundred, this surprising poem was a prompt commercial failure which its publisher, André Delpeuch, does not seem to have survived. I had the good fortune to rescue a few volumes of *Pour un Mauvais Garçon*, besides the one the author gave me. We are far here from the earlier works of Hélène Picard, from the *Instant éternel* crowned by the *Académie*, from *Nous n'irons plus au Bois*. . . . Where are the fountains and the moist moonlight, the muffled piano, everything that sobs and tinkles, so crystalline, in *Province et Capucines*? Where the most audacious verse — still so *jeune fille* — of the *Instant éternel* :

Je l'aimais tant qu'il me semblait l'avoir volé!

The fires of a personal hell glow in *Pour un Mauvais Garçon*. Berlioz might have called the strange still squall bearing away the hallucinated Hélène Picard '*Le voyage de Mephisto*'. But the poet decided that her Tempter should wear a checked cap and red pouch without his seductive powers being in any way thereby diminished. Thus he drags his blissful and tormented prey across a Baudelarian glory of pure-eyed demons and half-damned guardian angels. . . . What can we say? And what is there to fear? Nothing. We have here the magic of poetry, mirages, in short whatever comes most easily to a poet. Whatever, as a privileged confidante, I might interpret for the benefit of the strict and misleading truth I shall suppress. The truth never prevented Hélène from going to sleep every night in her small bed covered in the Virgin's colours. It was there, boarding her flying carpet, that she would run the gauntlet of the 'dens', cross the 'vile' thresholds, stroke the perfumed necks of the *mauvais garçons*; there it was that she would wake at first light, at the first cry from the chattering parakeets. . . .

She would have nothing to do with licentious books. Did she read much? The latter part of her life she shunned everything, even reading. Everything, except love and the expression of love. From what reverie flowed these lines, thrown on to a sheet of blue paper:

'At times you bend me like the vine which one begins to harvest and which resists. . . . At times you stretch me on the ground like a layer of ripe leaves and you lie down sighing on this shepherd's litter. . . .'

These grand divagations, these grand dissipations, amount to nothing, nothing but Poetry. Poetry alone possesses, seizes, lets fall, distributes to her eternal champions that which human love scatters so parsimoniously among its creatures.

Exuberant to a degree, Hélène, in conversation, seemed to have no secrets. But another aspect was that of solitude. One could hardly catch her unawares save at brief and furtive intervals, and when she allowed herself to plunge into deep reverie. What fierceness then on those so Latin features, moulded, recast by the expression of a mysterious fury. . . . Calmness would follow, as if from prudence, to extinguish this flame : 'Don't pay any attention, Colette! This is when I frighten children!' And her flinty eyes would regain their benevolent sparkle.

What were the targets of this mysterious anger, this launching of fluid and arrows? She was always brusque in her judgments, and ingenuously misogynous. Ingenuously, too, she would rejoice, as a savage, as an artist, in the charm emanating from some handsome passing plumber; she could say, in praise of a well-mannered man : 'He's almost as attractive as a delivery boy.' She might also say : 'That splendid butcher! Just look how attractive he is! And his crest of golden curls!' Her connoisseur's eulogy carried weight, a good peasant humour, the serenity of those who are capable of contemplating, face to face, the admirable and virile miracle that they esteem above all. Entirely, almost passionately, feminine, this literate Hélène would fall silent, embarrassed, when the talk around her was of homosexual perversions. She refused to concede that they might even exist. In connection with two women, who played the couple and whom we were judging without harshness, Hélène cried : 'No, no, it's ugly! Or it's only a joke. They're pretending, they're ridiculous.' One of us pointed out to her that the opposite sex was not exempt from or disdainful of analogous distractions. Hélène calmed down : 'Between boys, that's all right.' And when we protested in our turn, she could not or would not explain further. Again, in her masterpiece, *Pour un Mauvais Garçon*, the expression of her amorous fervour sometimes astonishes us when she speaks to the 'Unknown', her insubstantial lover :

> *Comme tu sens la fille et la nuit et la haie,*
> *Et peut-être, parfois, le bel enfant de choeur. . . .*

The august and impassioned scorn which is exhaled by such verses — she even goes so far as to call the idolized and disparaged lover *'ma chérie'* — scandalized even Carco :
'Hélène, Hélène, what you've written is outrageous!'
Hélène would give a wry smile and the poem would resume its enigmatic course under her hand :

> *Fais voir tes yeux dorés, dans cette fin de jour,*
> *Donne ta peau qui sent la rose at la vanille. . . .*
> *Et ton sourire, enfant, et ta main, pauvre fille,*
> *Tu es né sous le signe infame de l'amour.*

It is apparent that her mood, like the tone of her letters, darkened during her convalescence at the pretty Château du Val. Vain summer, unhelpful shade; I visit there a Hélène who is intolerant, rebellious as a student, irreverent towards the aged, even if they are ornamental, imposing former magistrates, still-young lieutenant-colonels, and she is bored at table. . . . She can stand it no longer, abandons the rheumatic Romeo with his two sticks, makes her escape, and returns to her small Parisian dwelling, where at least the dog-days are white and blue, where her window-ledge houses, between a clump of nasturtiums and the promises of a gladiolus, a minute kitchen-garden of garlic, thyme and parsley. But nothing now can prevent a baleful shadow from advancing towards her little by little, tarnishing her healthy rosy pallor, her tuberous pink. The attack was not confined to the bony damage, the very serious decalcification.

From what date did she resolve, overcome by aversion for the blood shed by animals, no longer to consume their flesh? Hélène did not tell me. She never gave herself away. Her bohemian subtlety easily outdid our own. The sudden and complete suspension of her meat diet, effected like an unimportant whim, threw her off balance, hastened the end. She, of course, disguised it as gourmandise, sang the virtues and fresh savour of raw mushrooms, pink radishes, leeks *en vinaigrette*, praised the feasts of salads, fruits, of cress with lemon. One day when I asked Hélène for her neglected succulent pork stew, she made an involuntary gesture of withdrawal : 'Forgive me, Colette, but *I can no longer* touch pork. . . .' Perhaps we, her friends, were not vigilant, not discerning enough, to track down and combat this mystical kind of revulsion. Only Professor Moreau knew a secret of which she was only partly aware. She allowed him to treat her for the deforming disease which began by bowing one tibia, then the other, then. . . .

'I have just,' she wrote to me, 'I have just had more than five hundred francs' worth of bolts fixed to my door. I am convinced, I am *morally* certain, that someone has been getting in.' She began to believe that someone was diverting her mail. She would trust only the *poste restante*. . . . Again she wrote: 'If I were not attached to this house by so many bonds, I should leave it, I have proof I am being spied on. But it would be the same, or worse, anywhere else. . . .'

Was this menacing cloud to grow even thicker? Hélène Picard had her remissions, she had not yet entirely lost her sense of the comic, her fresh mockery: 'My father and stepmother came from Foix to pay me a visit and I didn't know what to say to them. One interview every quarter of a century, that doesn't encourage conversation. They left eventually, leaving me . . . a little box of dry cakes.'

Prose, for her, was facile and of no account; her rapid sloping writing covered page after page in a few minutes. The invasive alexandrine gave rise to discarded material, thrust forward with insect feet, with pointed mandibles. . . . Active, sensitive, joyous writing which transmitted to me so many affectionate messages and childlike appeals for help: 'Help me, my own Colette! Once again I'm without any blue paper! Once again the ink at my stationer's has been diluted with the milky way! See how the nibs of my latest "sergeant-major" pen, brutalized by my . . . adjutant's fist, are crossed like the beak of the bird which is called — naturally! — the cross-beak. . . .'

That elegant sharp handwriting; its immateriality troubled me when the poet made use of it for her more glutinous verse, verse both winged and dense, burdened as if with a weight of flesh:

> *Toi qui fus ma bête et ma fleur,*
> *Et la jungle de ma caresse . . .*
> ....
> *Cette bassesse sourde, amoureuse et pâmée . . .*
> ....
> *Chaque fois que mes yeux s'abîmaient dans tes yeux,*
> *L'inceste nous frôlait de sa patte animale . . .*
> ....
> *Ton silence insolent, ta paresse légère,*
> *Et ton coeur pavoise, ô chaland des faubourgs!*
> ....

And this unlooked for threat, brutal rather than amorous:

> *Tu ne quitteras plus les hontes triomphales,*
> *Qu'inventa, cette nuit, mon vieux démon charnel.*

We falter over these two sombre lines, sensual and reticent, suited to the temperature which prevails in *Pour un Mauvais Garçon*. If it were a matter of another poet, I should have said that, when she wrote them, Hélène Picard had reached the age of authority, which often coincides with the stage of amorous exigence. But I should vouch that her 'season in hell' was not linked with any dishonourable gehenna. Let us rather entrust ourselves to the verbal freshness that abounds from her pen:

> *J'étais comme le vent incertain qui balance*
> *Une rose narquoise à la porte d'un bal....*

The direct threat of the war seems to have passed over the fragile roof of the rue d'Alleray without disturbing her who slept among the blue opalines and the great curtains of embroidered tulle. She believed only in those perils conjured from the past. From her flowered window-frame she followed the coloured trajectories in the sky and listened with a serene spirit to the gunfire, the chromatic alert. Only death could have interrupted the 'rosary of rhyme' strewn at each breath around Hélène Picard. Though she did not stir again, the remainder of her existence was a progressive and concerted evasion. This courageous woman flees, this vivid presence loses its substance; the wanderer, the habituée of remote suburbs, of colourful markets, little shops with gates and bell-pulls, grows static. . . . Worse still, she is fading away. She still suffers a benign ray of sunlight to touch her: the regard of an unknown, of a small local shopkeeper, of an errand-boy, these she admits in the darkness of a corridor, through a door she half opens. . . . She seems to be afraid of melting like rime in the warmth of affectionate commiseration. . . . I could wish not to have experienced the moment when the enemy's strength bore her down, bowed her to lean on two sticks, cast earthward that brown golden gaze enamoured of all that was elevated, winged, celestial; nevertheless, an ardent affection must attest that a poet died in hospital, in 1945, as one died in 1830.

Save for destitution, which she was spared, a cruel romanticism surrounded Hélène's ending; the hospital reduced to one communal ward (she had been discovered unconscious in her home and hurriedly removed), the prompt twilight of a winter's day, a coming and going of anonymous passers-by. Hélène died in such a setting, mute, evasive, terribly attached to her solitude. She died, and I think of her. How many friends have passed away whom I can call friends? Very few. Very few, thank God. How can one gauge friendship, save by its jewel-like rarity? When death intervenes, with its constancy of regret and its illumination, we can think: 'I loved truly.' The fine sentiment that risks being corrupted by physical illness, embittered old age, is restored by death to its pristine and faithful condition. . . . So that I can cherish Hélène anew without fear, severely, according to the example she used to set. For it was she who decided that our friendship had grown to become a bond which separation stretches but does not break, which is tested by its strength in absence, and which forms its judgments with uncompromising freedom. How many times have I heard Hélène abandon her scrupulous provincial protocol to emerge — the heel-thrust of the great diver — ablaze with paradox and arbitrariness, to comment gaily on some domestic crime. . . . I remember confessing to her some action I could have wished not to have committed, for which I reproached myself: 'Enough of these stories!' cried Hélène. 'For once you've been capable of a little greatness!'

It was this Hélène who lived in secret beneath the spangled cloak of Mme Hélène Picard, laureate in 1907 of a jury of women, as literate as they were *mondaines*. *Femina* boosted her to the level of the Baronne de Baye and Daniel Lesueur, not very far from a dinner photographed at Mme de Pierrebourg's, alias Claude Ferval. *Je sais tout* commemorated Hélène in evening dress, black tulle and jet, her hair in a coil round her forehead. Seated in a photographer's armchair, she holds, so as to bear witness to her literary status, a large open album. . . .

I've no other means now of being with her than to talk to myself about her. My husband hardly had more than a glimpse of her. She welcomed him from the height of our long friendship, with a circumspect gentleness which conferred on the presence of this best friend beside me a character, shall I say episodic, which he has been able to resent in silence. Our friends find it difficult enough to like our friends.

Seven

I've done no work today. Writing is often wasteful. If I counted the pages I've torn up, of how many volumes am I the author? Lucie Delarue-Mardrus, who has also just died, had the good fortune to attack all her work with an overwhelming dash. Rheumatism twisted this valiant performer in every direction and put her on the rack. I found her ever ready to pour out verse and prose, speak in public, study Latin, model in wax, string a melody on a five-lined stave. . . . She enjoyed correcting my texts, without malice, when she thought they required it. 'I expect you're very proud,' she wrote to me from Château-Gontier, 'because you've stuck the word *anatife** in your latest book to astound us. Well, too bad for you, but you must say *inventiver contre* and *tâcher à. . . .*'

I could wish that she were still among us, busy lecturing to me. I thought of her when I was writing the word *pholade.*† She would have reprimanded me for it in her child's voice, looking down from the height of her little head with its great slow eyes, its artless and turned-up nose which pulled her lip upwards. . . .

'Aren't you ever short of subjects for novels?' I once asked her.

'I've over a hundred, over two hundred, three hundred,' she replied. 'Do you want any? I'll give you as many as you like. Come and see my new apartment. Come and see my carved candles. Come and see my models for a puppet theatre. . . .'

We separated and all was silence between us for months. It was not our fault.

She, too, had cut her abundant brown hair, the thick tresses that she wore for so long braided round her head. My hair, a metre fifty-eight long, the silver straw which wreathed the

---

* Barnacle.
† A mollusc — the piddock or stone-borer. (Tr.)

forehead of the Amazon, what a harvest reaped by whim, by fashion. . . . At least the widow of the Duc de Morny, around 1867, had strewn her hair on her husband's coffin, and her gesture, heralded by the sound of horns, preserved an air of loving sacrifice. . . .

'Oh, how I wish people would shut up about my mother's sacrifice,' grumbled Mathilde, known as Missy, the Duke's youngest daughter. 'For two years she pestered my father to let her wear her hair short and he strictly forbade her. She certainly got away with it!'

They are very various, the guilty pleasures of widows.

'A black veil, and underneath a monkey's smile,' as my mother used to say.

It has grown late, without my having noticed it. It is the hour which is often said to be particularly long and gloomy for elderly lonely persons. Yet two hours, three hours are to me like moments, so long as a relative indolence comes to my aid. Working, the time drags, the quarters of an hour are chewed with difficulty, like hunks of coarse bread eaten without drinking or salivating. This afternoon I had a quiet day, passed in idling and suffering. Near me, in the blue of the evening, there still gleams the watch with the golden dial which I call my cardiac watch because, hanging by its ring from a nail as slender as a pin, the beating of my heart makes it oscillate gently. It measures out my life but it is I who keep it going. If I forget to wind it even for one day, it will fall silent, overtaken by death. Who could repair it? It is old, the skilled craftsmen who could have looked after it are dead too. I can see that, one of these days, I shall have to see it acquire the melancholy status of an *objet d'art*. . . .

Behind the frosted glass that takes the place — poorly — of a wall between the two rooms I inhabit a yellow glow has just lit up. Now it's time all at once to suffer less, to make up one's face rather better, to listen to the telephone, a premonitory clashing of plates, and rings at the bell which excite only defiance, mockery and hilarity. On some days I go so far as to say, inwardly : 'Sh . . . on all these bells, but *now*!' But these are out-bursts of irreverence that do not last. . . .

I had barred my door, this afternoon, in honour of a visitor who had come from her suburb at considerable inconvenience, a little woman of about sixty, rather dumpy, dressed in rusty black. She is a 'home clairvoyant'; a rather timid clairvoyant who must be frightened by the phantoms she conjures up. It was our first encounter and she immediately warned me honestly :

'You know, madame, I don't always *see*. When I don't *see*, I prefer to say so right away, right? My *clientèle* consists mainly of people who can't get about, so I can come back again. Do you want me to ask you questions or shall I just tell you what I see?'

I preferred to abandon myself to her clairvoyance and she removed her gloves from hands worn by housework. For a quarter of an hour no dazzling light was shone on either my past or my present. Illness, vexations, estrangements, successes, removals — the small change of prophecy poured out and my little clairvoy-ant excused herself like a singer who feels out of voice. I was sorry for her, I could have wished to prompt her. . . . I offered her a hot infusion. She thanked me with a kindly tentative look from her eyes, bluish and bulging as were those of the celebrated and defunct Elise, 'the woman with the candle'. For a moment she leaned forward, appearing to look for something on the carpet.

'Have you dropped your glove?'

She did not reply but went on looking :

'Ah!' she said, 'it's a cat.'

'What?'

'It's a cat.'

'You see a cat?'

'Yes, it's just gone under your chair and mine. For a moment I said to myself : "What can that be?" It's a cat.'

'Why not a tomcat?'

She made a gesture of ignorance.

'I don't know, madame. "A cat" is what they tell me.'

'What's she like?'

88

'Oh, she's not very pretty! . . . I mean she's not like those fine big long-haired cats. . . . She's grey all over.'

'Can you see her now?'

'Yes. There's no problem, she's there all the time. She doesn't want to leave you. You mean everything to her.'

'Can you see her move about?'

'Certainly. She comes and goes, she walks around. She does what she likes because she's dead.'

'Do you know how long she's been dead?'

'No.'

She corrected herself, adding immediately:

'It's four years now.'

'But you just said you knew nothing about it.'

'I didn't know anything, *someone* has just told me.'

'Is it a voice you hear?'

The honest seer gave me an imploring look:

'Yes. . . . No, it's not an ordinary voice, I don't hear any words, but I grasp the meaning. . . . I'm not very good at explaining myself. . . .'

She would accept only a modest sum and I let her go. I told my best friend about her visit when he got back and our discussion thereon, as can be imagined, centred on the presence of the Cat, the Last Cat, the one of whom we used to say: 'What the Cat doesn't know isn't worth knowing.' If her soul, got up to look 'grey all over', still haunts our dwelling four years after death, visible only to eyes sensitive to the invisible, then it's because we have remained worthy of her. We shan't forget those consoling words: 'She does what she likes, because she's dead.' And I shall take care never to summon the humble seer again for fear of learning from her lips that the Cat, this time, has left us for good.

I don't recall ever in my life having consulted more than four or five persons gifted with second sight. But it pleases me to recognize that their diverse gifts are able to disconcert our human sight. If the future — my own — had ever made me curious, I might have sought more frequent meetings with these exceptional persons.

My first contact with the occult came about when, at her request, I accompanied one of those young women who are feminine to the point of shunning anything masculine, including therein men themselves. A wounded dove, a wilting flower, incited by the vogue for *Aphrodite* and the *Chansons de Bilitis* to certain moral indiscretions. Unknown to her Myrtocleia, this sensitive Rhodis requested my reassuring presence at a 'highly born' Russian's, named Saphira, whose gaze, according to her, 'pierced' the future and the past, not to mention the present.

Reality revealed an elderly man, made up and reeking of perfume. His clients, if any of them remain, cannot have forgotten his very beautiful eyes, whose pupils were surrounded by two concentric rings of velvet blue. 'Don't leave me alone with him, I'm frightened!' said Rhodis. I did as she wished and we awaited the oracle — not for long. The soothsayer bent his great height over the young woman and said abruptly :

'Beware! You're going to a man! Beware! There is danger. I tell you, there is danger!'

The effect of this prediction was unforeseen. Rhodis got up and with the air of a woman who has just had her bottom pinched in the Métro, burst forth with :

'Why, monsieur! But not at all! It's a slander, monsieur! I won't allow you. . . .'

I think, red as she was, that she would have left without paying if Saphira had not demanded a sizeable fee, as befitted a Russian of noble origin.

The very next day a gossiping, slanderous, fearful, curious little world squawked the news : Rhodis had just run off with a handsome young man. Myrto made herself ridiculous by pursuing the heterosexual couple, fired off a couple of unskilful revolver shots, and everything settled down.

Who can give me the key to Saphira? How is one to disentangle, from a mass of tinsel, banality and Slav origins, from a name borrowed from the Kabbala, from make-up, large rings, a wasp-waisted frock-coat whatever he could lay claim to of authentic lucidity and sorcery, to use the word I find most satisfactory? Who will enlighten me on a reader of cards, who used to be called 'the good wife of the rue de Chazelles?' She seemed, one day, very intrigued herself by what the tarot cards showed and repeated, as if her client could have done something about it: 'See, there is a person who is a long way away, a child rather, thirteen or fourteen years old, who is moving about a lot. But what can he hope to achieve by moving about so much? I can't see. . . . But someone ought to tell him not to create such a disturbance!'

Three days later the young man 'a long way away', who went riding on horseback every day, fell and was confined to bed for three months. The fanatic client did not wait three months to return to the rue de Chazelles, where the seer rewarded her with nothing but senseless remarks. Repetition is as valueless to clairvoyants as to poisonous snakes. Strange ability to uncover what is hidden or to furnish venom, when both are exhausted by repetition. It is this exhaustion that makes for deceit. A medium counterfeits, a clairvoyant improvises, for fear of proving inferior to their genuine gift.

Only Elise and the 'sleeping woman', both of the rue Caulaincourt, rent the veil of the future, and with assured hands. But then the sleeper died, worn out and cadaverous from the slumbers demanded of her. The astounding 'woman with the candle', Elise, underwent an eclipse which desolated the faithful:

'Do you know what, Elise can't *see* any more! It's a calamity!'

'Impossible! What's happened to her?'

'She's taken up with a curé and all at once she can't see any more in the candle.'

A joyful verbal publicity announced the restoration of the wonder-working:

'You know, she's not with the curé any more. All of a sudden she can see again in the candle!'

For many years Elise, with the end of a kitchen-knife, exploited the candle that her clients used to bring between skin and chemise, and that she held, inclined and lighted, over a plate. Peremptory, foul-mouthed, capricious as a wild ass, Elise would speak, or not speak. She would open the door of her small apartment herself. 'Is Madame Elise at home?' A look — the pop-eyed glaucous gaze that seemed overcome by myopia — and Elise would reply: 'No!' or, more gently, 'Go ahead, come in.'

She scraped the melting wax that spilled from the lighted candle. She teased the wick, which became long and black. She wandered incoercible among unexpected deaths, hidden illnesses, accused events which would remain dormant and disguised for years to come. If her client, sometimes taken aback, did not implore her silence she would continue to overflow with whining and coarse expressions, with 'You don't half give me a headache!' or 'I don't care a fuck for any of that!', with details of a barely believable crudity and infallibility (fact):

'A fine marriage. Yes, there'll be a marriage. But as for children, that's another matter. No kids.'

'Why, madame Elise?'

'Because the young man has poor spunk.'

I soften the expressions. . . .

I once had the good fortune to hear Elise — every great artiste has his moment of triumph — amble through four years of the future, describing accurately, naming misfortunes, announcing an imminent drama 'in a country beyond the sea. . . .' (Chevandier de Valdrôme was assassinated by his cook in Casablanca), the inheritance that would follow, the financial problems:

'Ah, what lawsuits there's going to be! For three million, no more, no less, there now, that'll teach him, that one, to buy so many foreign bonds! It's the same with this young girl, they're off for a spree at the spas, much good that'll do them! She'll get hold of his three millions in the end, but can she hang on to them, eh? Three, four years and then, in the can! She's had it all right, she's had it.'

She smiled into space, above the plateful of congealing wax.

'They don't know anything about it, not them.'

Suddenly, at the height of her prophetic fire, she would fall silent, yawn noisily, press her forehead, and wipe her swollen eyes with a corner of her apron. Painfully she would return to earth among us. . . .

I was introduced to her, at the beginning of the '14-18 war, by Mme Paul Iribe, the first of that name. This beautiful young woman, Jeanne Dirys, intelligent but without talent, tried her hand in the theatre, in business and in marriage with incorrigibly bad luck. Accustomed to Elise's infallibility, she often made an appearance at the rue Caulaincourt, as she might have visited an opium den. But opium lies sometimes, and Elise fuddled her with the truth. Far from employing the wily modes of information to which minor soothsayers resort, Elise refused to know the names of her clients, the names of countries and towns, or portraits. She wore her mystery entire, her waggish humour, the disordered knowledge she had of our destinies, her brief charity : 'When I'm talking to someone I predict everything, except death,' she used to say. She would add, with a disdain clothed in frankness : 'They'll stand anything but that.'

Whom else should I think about, peaceful and solitary, if not the transients of my life, those passers-by whose illegible but firm outline permits neither explanation nor forgetfulness?

The sleeping woman of the rue Caulaincourt was far from the level, the everyday level, of Elise. She was a poor little grub with a face the colour of a blanched salad, barely alive between two slumbers. Asleep, she fell at once into an invalid posture, twisted over to one side like some of the children at Berck, her neck all crooked. To get her to speak it was necessary to hold one of her soft, boneless, inexpressive hands. Apart from the oracles in her little girl's voice, her appearance and her touch frightened the timid. But the dismaying unvarnished future truth had chosen to pass through that wretched body, and pass it did, unpityingly. It wandered therein, blocked by islets, held up at every turn of its course, slowly disgorged, mingled with the crackle and smell of the onions that one could hear frying in a small adjacent kitchen.

93

As well as the need to see only a very few faces, to hear a small number of voices, there takes shape, paradoxically, the need to decipher this fine masked design for which a pair of eyes, a solitary nose and mouth suffice. It's in the light of this thirst, this minimum of sociability, that I let anyone in. And then, the old politeness, learned and never forgotten, which insists on one salutation being answered by another, on the consent to a request. . . . The glazed door of the 'bull-pen' half opens, the stranger enters. . . . He has his purpose. His weapons are inquiry, the request for an article, simple curiosity, a business proposition. Since the war I know nothing of him or her, while they have an old stereotyped image of me. He tells me, she assures me, that a very important journal, due to 'come out' soon, would like to know. . . . They imagine that I could not forbear to burst forth on the world with an opinion on votes for women, the purge, the role of the young girl in the new order, reform of the theatre, the closing of restaurants, the questions of paper and housing. He asks, she begs, for an account of my literary projects. . . .

There they are, on the edge of the divan which I use for working and being ill, the divan-raft on which I've floated for so many years. They're seated on those small tapestry-work chairs which I enjoyed covering with an old design, which testify to a well-ordered solitude. And for a time allotted, fortunately by me, I am their prisoner. Appearing to find their presence natural, it is I who feel on trial. What can be more normal than to quake in the presence of the young? Maybe they too are inwardly uneasy. They think that I have some general ideas. It is not for me to inform them that I exist on those funds of frivolity that come to the aid of the long-lived. That a time comes when one has to choose between bitterness, pessimism as it used to be called, and its opposite, and that my choice was made long

94

since — or let us say, more accurately, that it is flaunted.

I have no other recourse, where they are concerned, than to stare at them. It's a difficult profession they've embarked on. The war has not taught them anything about it. Their ingenuousness shows through their offhand manner and it may well be that their assurance is as deceptive as my own. Not that it prevents them from having the great advantage of manipulating the question-mark, an aggressor's weapon. I can interrogate only their faces. What is the origin of that precocious wrinkle? Of that scar round the neck? Of that forlorn look in so young a person? Of that profound fatigue betrayed by frequent long respirations?

'Would it be tactless, madame, to. . . .'

Of course. Before the end of the sentence I know perfectly well that it will be tactless.

'And among your literary projects, madame, are you. . . .'

The speaker is twenty-two or twenty-three years old, with the volubility of an old stager, a blond curl that falls over his eyes. If I did not see his fountain-pen shaking I might take him for self-assurance personified. Plans, my lad? But of course. At sixty-three years of age, less a quarter, one still has plans. I've no lack of them. I plan to live a little longer yet, to continue to suffer in honourable fashion, that is without complaint or rancour, to rest my gaze on faces like yours — you look like my daughter a little bit — to laugh quietly to myself and also to laugh openly when there's cause, to love those who love me, to put in order what I shall leave behind me, the bank deposit as well as the drawer of old photographs, a little linen, the few letters. . . . But these plans are not for you. And I reply to you gravely, young man charged to investigate, responsible so young :

'My plans. . . . Hmm. . . . I don't want to talk about them for a few months. . . . No, no. . . . By that time possibly a volume of memoirs. . . . As for the novel. . . . Oh, no! I couldn't tell you anything about my method of working. . . .'

I keep a straight face. He makes a note. I add a few hesitant words, a gesture, behind which he may choose to descry an expanse of great thoughts. . . . There, it's over. He goes off with

95

a piece of American chocolate I've given him making a bulge in his cheek. He leaves by the wrong door — Pauline has gone out — he enters a little shower-room and apologizes to it, he enters the glacial little room with a glass ceiling which lets in the rain, wanders into the lavatory in the hall, tries to close behind him the front-door which only obeys a password — in short he's gone and I am left to ponder on what that young hanger-on calls my method of work. 'Perhaps you might have among your notes, madame. . . .'

He seemed to find it quite natural that I should have a method of work, and even that I might wish to keep it secret. He himself certainly has one . . . I should have interviewed *him*. . . .

Among my notes. . . . What notes? I shan't leave a single one behind me. Oh, I've tried! Everything I wrote down became as sad as the skin of a dead frog, sad as a plan for a novel. On the strength of those writers who do make notes, I had made notes on a sheet of paper, and lost the paper. So I bought a notebook, American style, and lost the notebook, after which I felt free, forgetful, and willing to answer for my forgetfulness.

Not a note, not a notebook, not the least little scrawled indication. Whence, then, were derived my anonymous heroes? The first of them all, that Renaud whom Claudine married, is inconsistency itself. This ripe seducer, born of the imagination of a young woman still girlish enough to believe in ripe seducers, I had no sooner created him than I took a dislike to him, and as soon as he gave me the chance I killed him off. His death gave me the feeling of having attained a kind of literary puberty, a foretaste of those delights allowed to the praying mantis.

But the Maxime of *La Vagabonde*, the Jean of *L'Entrave*, were hardly any better. Neither of these two transcends the level of the male extra. Not knowing how to deal with my own inadequacies I condemned them to idleness and allotted them as fields of action only the bed or the divan. Sensuality is no career for an honest man. I did not venture again to depict lovers devoid of scruples.

With Farou, of *La Seconde*, I felt rather more at ease and my fine fellow was less artificial. Cosily ensconced between wife

Colette at the window of her Palais-Royal apartment in Paris.

Colette and Maurice Goudeket in their apartment at the Palais-Royal.

and mistress, Farou leans against both, acquiring a little life from two female rivals who do not hate each other. Who have not hated each other. Who will not hate each other. Who grow old with a high opinion of each other, without ever completely forgetting the contempt they had nursed for the man's peculiar cowardice. . . . So-called *roman à clef*, how you tempt us! How you incite our pen, not to deny, but to establish the sentimental truth which binds two women and their tolerable unhappiness in the service of one man!

Young man, I should have answered you: 'Yes, I have met Chéri. We have all met Chéri, endowed with his meteoric characteristics.' Perhaps you wished, young man, vaguely disturbed, to go into what you privately call 'the story of a gigolo'. The word ages gracelessly, evokes I don't know what nervous tic. Why not 'diabolo'? Why should a young demon not boast a name as amiable and charged with menace as himself? The story of a diabolo. . . .

Oh yes, I've met Chéri, more than once, just as I've met other temptations. To every woman her own trouble, and the comparison she makes of it with different troubles. No doubt I shan't make myself well understood if I say that, for me, Chéri has a symphonic value. His mutism conveys the disintegrating power of music, borrows disorder from instrumental and, especially, vocal timbres. A voice — such a voice! — that rose from an Italian tenor, ugly, old and fat. . . . Another voice which emanated, very improbably, from a Prussian singer named, barring orthographic error, Von zür Mühlen, a worn, feeble, almost exhausted voice which sang very rarely in Paris around 1900; after an hour's concert he would dismiss a red-eyed audience. The career of a great neurotic artist is brief; this one began to detect, in every gathering of music-lovers, a man or woman with the evil eye and every time he would refuse to sing or stop in the middle.

The link between Chéri and music appears less close when Chéri sings out of tune. If he sang in tune, his charm — using the word charm here in its malefic sense — would be definable, even admissible. I do Chéri the honour of comparing him to music only because the latter is the delectable agent of all melancholy. Potent, incomplete, Chéri is *par excellence* the one who can make a well-informed woman, orientated towards precise goals, lose her great gusty laughter, her gaiety and assurance. From the moment when she realizes that Chéri, even in subjection, is not a case of appetite alone, that, though useless, he is yet irreplaceable, that a glow, an expression, a feature, mysterious as an indecipherable signature, are affixed to him, generic and tenacious, she still has time to accept or decline the danger.

I could not wholeheartedly affirm that the Chéri, the *'fils Peloux'*, of my novel resembled anyone. But I should lie if I said that he resembled no one. In the presence of such a young man, silent, grave, mistrustful, admired, I have thought: 'In tears he would be even more beautiful.' But I did not imagine that I should be able to make him shed these tears. He whom, in my novel, I call 'the inaccessible bearer of light', whom I endow with 'an illiterate majesty', keeps us at a distance, even after our embrace, with an unspoken *noli me tangere*, by subsiding into a silence which is, perhaps, a premature mourning for his own beauty. Chéri is no more capable of eloquence than of laughter. Attacked at his weak points by his audacious partner, it is by silence that he regains his arrogance.

I speak of him with an authority that I do not mistake for infallibility.

Thus it was that I patiently dealt with the various queries of the fair-haired reporter. If people talk to me about Chéri and his fate, or about Sido, I exhibit competence and complacency. I know where my best work as a writer is to be found.

At one point it seemed to me that the young reporter overstepped the bounds of his mission. 'Madame, did Chéri . . .' — he blushed, which made him look three or four years younger — '. . . did Chéri ever exist?' He realized that, even for a journalist in 1945, the question was rather pointed. It's of no importance to establish whether, in some place or other, a very old young man, now bent and grey, escaped the suicide I inflicted on Chéri. But it pleases me that my youth of obscure birth, with the melancholy of a very handsome man which constrains him, finally, to a barren purity, should have influenced a wide public, if only by tickling their curiosity.

It once happened, in the course of a lecture tour, that I arrived at a spa where I was welcomed to the station by an unexpected chattering and charming group of young girls who had spontaneously delegated themselves to meet me. Speaking at the tops of their voices and all at once, they eagerly imparted a great secret:

'Madame, we've got Chéri! Yes, madame, we've had Chéri in person for some days now. We're mad about him! Anyway, if you come to tea with us — oh do! oh do! — you'll see him go by, it's his time for tennis, you'll recognize him right away, it's Chéri himself!'

Naturally I did as they wished and I saw their Chéri, who was certainly not mine, or Léa's. If I kept silent, it was not from admiration. But that everyone should model Chéri in their own fashion, isn't that just what I wanted?

He received more than praise, the 'naughty child' whom I laid on Léa's bosom. Men were hard on him, especially those whose youth had departed. Those most affected by the great evil of age showered me from above with words of severe and disinterested disapproval:

'What can you be thinking of, my dear,' said one of them, 'to want to draw our attention to a type as exceptional, not to say improbable, as your Chéri? And those people, those whores, those. . . .'

Instead of reacting like a chestnut in the fire, I kept quiet. I acknowledged that virtuous masculine incompetence might treat a lover devastated by a unique love as a 'pale gigolo', and a 'leech-like queer'. For the first time in my life I felt morally certain of having written a novel for which I need neither blush nor doubt, a novel whose appearance massed partisans and critics round it.

And I was able to put on airs in obtaining my reward from women alone, when Chéri became a success. Here I evoke the phalanx of 'Léas', masked combatants, invincible, bare of face and breast. . . . They had an indescribable way of recognizing each other, of applauding me and becoming my friends, of showing their fealty in a look, a squeeze of the hand. The most beautiful, the closest also to her total ruin, once wordlessly cried to me the 'Ah yes, yes!' with which Balzac scorched the lips of Veronique Greslin, lover of a Chéri as young and culpable. . . . Another, full-blown, like a rose crumpled under the weight of a happiness whose hours were numbered, profited from a solitary moment to tell me 'all' in three words rendered disarming by a smile, a sigh:

'Ah, the swine. . . .'

She departed. She wore a blue mohair dress, like Léa, a leaden blue that went very well with her grey-blue goura's crest,* and thanks to her long skirt no one noticed that her ankles were swollen. . . .

See how the visit of this young sprig of a journalist has taken me back with his determination to talk to me of plans and future! Who will succeed him on the edge of my boat?

Come in, it's the appointed time, you whom I call my idleness and my recreation. Come in, just a few. Come in, you who scratch at my door to spare me the shock, the alarm of the bell, you whom I do not name, whom I do not describe, whom I do not despise, whom I respect. Come in with your rubber boots or your fine tailor-made costume, your woollen scarf round a muzzle frozen by the wind of your bicycle. Don't be afraid of me, neither your name nor your story will be found in these pages. Come in, still braced and dazzled by music, you who have suffered melting snow and wintry blast to hear a fine concert. Come in, you who run in search, every day, for what you and yours need. Put down your inseparable basket, let's extol the clandestine slice of hake, veal chop or coffee; let's share the dirty trick of honest folk embroiled in the foul traffic, since one must eat. Come in, you who travel from the steppes of Neuilly for me, just for me!

Come in, my neighbour the poet, my neighbour the play-wright, my neighbour the scenario-writer, my neighbour the

* The goura (Goura coronata) is a large crested pigeon of New Guinea and adjacent islands. (Tr.)

painter, come in all of you in a single personage — like a grey-hound, tall and mobile. You are like those shrimps of translucent agate, the colour of water save for the last little alga they've swallowed; one can see your alga inside you : a five-pointed star.

Come in pairs, my charming frock-coated doctors, exclaim how well I look; in exchange I'll let fall some brief remarks on your professional fatigue, unmatchable prescriptions, advice on régimes. Come in, yet another, turn round so that I may see your new dress, your lumber-jacket lined with real sheepskin. There slip in among you one or two men who always have an habitual air of jays surrounded by a flock of tits. It's because you're alive and still such as the war has fashioned you, prompt in decision, quick in talk, glad henceforward to contradict the opinions of the man you protected. . . .

Talk to me about the cinema, about painting. I'll read you the latest letter from the wives of the small farmers, alone on their flat Normandy earth, who struggle for their existence and that of their livestock, reduced almost to nothing, read in the snow the delicate tracks of the hen-stealing fox and his busy brush, deliver the cow at three o'clock in the morning in the great silence. Not a man on the farm, not a man to fork the litter, to saw the wood, tend the colic of the aged horse. . . . Two women, as solitary as if they were on a reef. . . . Let us admire and pity them; before you go, warm your little cold paws under my stuffed quilt. A moment more. . . . 'Let me tell you about. . . .' We know how to laugh, and very well. But just a word, the mention of a date, an anec-dote, and there reappears fleetingly on our faces the old expression of the women you were — destitute, hunted, partnerless. . . . If one of you here should be called to the telephone, she stops laughing, she coughs as if something had gone down the wrong way, she says in a feeble little voice: 'Oh dear, what can they want of me?' She, no more than I, likes the doorbell, the clock striking, loudspeakers, sirens. A whole family of sonorities has become hateful to us, since. . . .

Nine

Night, O Night, sighs the Arab chant, O thou Night once more. . . . When I embark on night in the name of rest and, if possible, sleep, she is already half-engaged in her course towards the limpidity of morning. We go to bed very late, my companion and I. But how to limit the length and seduction of these evenings that make us aware of the solidity, the substance, the silence of Paris? It is midnight, one o'clock, half past one. . . . Our routine eventually separates us, obedient to its rites. 'Yes, I've bolted the front-door.' But as the door doesn't hold fast. . . . Never mind, it's best to bolt it. 'If you don't feel well, give me a call.' I swear to do so. But this oath is only a codicil to a pre-existing convention which commands respect for a neighbour's sleep. Respect for this — to me — so surprising form of complete repose : the creature which, going to sleep at night, neither stirs nor opens its eyes till the following morning. Once I had to shake my best friend out of his long and deep slumber, from which he emerged with a start, and I had the time to observe on his forcibly reopened face that his startled awakening will doubtless always bear the date of December 12th, 1941. . . .

The door closed between us, I am free not to sleep, to wander around a little, to limp unconcealedly, to go and eat what's left of the marmalade. There's no noise to give me away, I've charmed the latches and hinges long since.

I hesitate to call those nights bad that the arthritis chooses to torment my leg and hip. There is, in the pain that comes in bursts or waves, an element of rhythm which I cannot entirely condemn, a flux and reflux whose autonomy grips the attention. What I call honourable suffering is my dialogue with the presence of this evil. Standing, it stops me from walking, but lying down I can hold my own against it. The proof lies in the absence from my bed-table of any analgesic or hypnotic drug. Pain, save for a few rare failures of my will, I've waited for you to withdraw from this limb you torment and you've withdrawn. You've not yet succeeded in making a morass of my awakening, my tongue bitter, my sleep clouded with pale and suspect marvels. . . .

It's not forbidden to read at night, when one is ill. But it's rather like being a spoilt child, seeking to shorten the night's darkness. Darkness or slumber, which is the most pressing? 'Have the maximum number of sunny hours', counsels hygiene. If this is to the detriment of the dark hours, I protest. The night has its various needs, and insomnia satisfies at least one of these if we do not insult it with great parade of lamp and book. Are we so tormented by remorse or grief that the shade becomes our enemy, and the night-bird can only tolerate a night wounded by a thousand lights? My mother used to tell me ('Off we go again,' as Lucie Delarue-Mardrus might have said. 'We're back to her mother already, her cat can't be far away!') with astonishment that my elder half-sister, when she was young, was infatuated with the night, during which she neither slept nor cried but 'thought' in her cradle. Her blank eyes, wide open, contemplated the darkness with a precocious air of vigilance and good humour, and as she grew up she remained faithful to the shadow.

The lamp relit at my bed-table, I reproach myself for having suppressed those points of light which — in the absence of the big moon — the small moon, Vesper, and the stars grant us after dark over Paris. A kind of dawn haloes the Conseil d'État, betrays beyond it the lighted regions of the city. In the beautiful blue-black tinges of my room a luminous wand attaches itself to the hands of a watch. Another, as I've said, climbs the cruppers of the little gilt horse. If I press the switch of my lamp my feeble landmarks, pensive, ranged like the lights of a village, will be eclipsed and the white slab of the book will shine out. . . . I prefer, visible through the gap of the half-open window, a green signal, another desk-lamp, suspended at the very end of the Galerie Montpensier. . . . When the pleasanter season of 'sleeping in the garden' arrives — and it is due — my starboard light will be seen, in its turn, by that other pilot-light down there. Grave guardians of my night. . . . It's from them that, immobile in the depths of my obscurity, I asked for the *Story of the Sick Child*. Little by little, they granted it to me. I invented the child and, for the rest, I went from the green lantern to the golden rings that intertwine when one is half-asleep. . . . What can no longer be worked out as a novel can be managed for eighty pages.

Were it not for this arthritic illness, I should not have got to know those who look after me. Before then, I'd never given a thought to doctors. In the past, when I was ill, they used to trust me. If I had influenza or bronchitis they would address me politely over the telephone: 'Yes, yes, I see, you've been careless again. Now you know as well as I do, my dear, what needs to be done. . . . That's right, cupping-glasses at the back, poultices in front . . . aspirin. . . . Fine! . . . Hot drinks can't do any harm. . . . And ring me about your temperature this evening!'

Their seeming indifference was a tribute to my robustness. But now, because of this increasingly handicapped and painful limb, because of my age, they come without my sending for them and insist on looking after me almost against my will. They have determined, if not to cure me, at least that I shan't suffer any more. They devote to this a private passion which fills me with delight, not for any hope this may give me but as an index of their affection. The long hollow needle, masterfully inserted in the crease of the groin, the gold pin stuck in Chinese style into the little toe, behind the heel or at the level of the kidneys, and the 'rays' — I see in these the material emblems of a magic spell. For real relief there's something much better, there is the spoken word, the warm hand, the zeal of an individual who, full of his science and overburdened with work, pretends when he is with me to be idle, dawdles, turns the pages of a book, lingers, talks. . . . Forehead against the window, he contemplates the garden of the Palais-Royal, seems to forget me. . . . Delicious deception, his back watches me, his neck listens to me, his care envelops me. O great man who has remained generous, continue to hold my hand, lay on my cheek your own rough cheek, shaven at dawn, when you say goodbye. Ask me, as if you were greedy, for a cup of coffee; thus you can feel sure that I shall do you credit and that, after the treatment, a cup of coffee will save me from

transient giddiness or dizziness. And see how you love me enough
to give me, if I beg for them, the drops, the pills, the lozenges
that pain grasps at so eagerly and digests, exhausted, like an
insect overcome by formalin vapour. See how you think to yourself: 'She really deserves this respite.' But I don't ask you for
them. I reject them even. I've two small tubes here, one of
gardenal, the other of dial, still unopened after thirty-four years.
I had depended on them once to get rid of a female complaint
which was like a good many female complaints. The two little
poisons are still sealed. Their intact seal marked the beginning
of my defiance, and the distinction I insist on making — I, who
cannot face the dentist without a gum full of novocaine —
between useful and unnecessary pain. I insist and you shrug your
shoulders, you friends who lead me to believe that the medical
profession is recruited from the saints. In these February days,
when winter melts and becomes sunny, one of you, some man
or woman, will come in:

'It's only twelve, I can spare a good half-hour. It's mild out,
I'll take you in the car round the Île Saint-Louis. The forsythias
are out in the flower market, the sparrows are running like rats
among the pots of myrtle. . . . Let's go, let's go!'

Let's go! We'll go, here and there, to see Paris. We'll go
alongside a hedge of barrows whose appearance, odour and
greenery create an illusion of a food market. We'll go to gaze at
the rainy mauve, the misty blue, created by paulownias about to
blossom. We'll go to look at Hermes' window, for the sake of a
purple and grey scarf, a broad old red-and-pink ribbon, a shim-
mering grouping on a violet background of the dormant fire of
faded flowers, a cluster of golden jewels, scaly as fishes. . . . We'll
go to the rue des Archives, where, at the centre of a quadrangle
of narrow huddled arches, a Parisian tree, frail and enduring,
glitters with buds like a jetting fountain with drops. . . .

We'll go. Meanwhile I drink in the sea breeze that mounts
from the Seine; and beside me I sense the stirring, beneath the
impressive medical exterior, of the precious gift to perceive and
wordlessly to pity human suffering.

105

Tonight I dreamed that I was on horseback, with stirrups that were a little too long. The delightful swaying, the joy of galloping on a well-worn saddle, the pleasure of feeling a sensitive mouth with my light hand, my dream restored everything of which I had been long deprived. But the probing malignity of reality was not long in returning. I was made aware that I should have to dismount, in order to shorten my stirrups a notch. 'But if I get down, I shan't be able to get into the saddle again *because of my leg*.' An observation too judicious to be acceptable to the logic of a dream; I woke up.

When I dream — I dream but little — I very often delight in what my waking hours wisely deprive me of. If I were to regain the use of my leg, I should go to a boxing-match. I should go and sit in the front row at a wrestling bout. I should go to see a film of some great horse-race, I should go to share, with a muscled rhythm of legs or shoulders, the impact of the fists, the contraction of the loins, the gallop. . . . In dreams I do so.

A few, the choicest, dreams compile a miscellany of places unbeholden to reality, with its more tedious details. A dream occurred one night, then returned again, in such a way that, making my way at night towards a real place, I recognized the staircase of a house in the rue des Courcelles, and its wallpaper in raw jute. But my nights reveal it printed with lions of periwinkle blue, beset with oak balusters, with treads and hand-rails of oak; a forest of oaks, sacrificed to an 1890 staircase. . . . The periwinkle lions are pure creatures of dream, held fast in their oneiric alignment by the most authentic plinths and stylobates in the world. Periwinkle blue, rimmed with a grey-blue border, the mouth heraldically gaping, the tongue a marine helix. More or less upright, they have a heavy open forepaw. Rather English lions, in fact. How lucky that I can't draw. I'd stick them in my margins for you, faithful copies of non-existent figures. I take them for granted now, they serve as a firm link, an indispensable complement, to that pattern which is reality.

One of my colleagues, and not the least of them, has declared that I have no imagination. Now that's a fine state of affairs, if it's true. But what would he say to Mallarmé, quoted by Henri

Mondor? 'In the depth of the dream, perhaps, there strives the imagination of those who deny it its daytime flight. . . .' For sixty years I have peacefully scoured my countryside to flush out one more harvest, another cat or chicken, a twilight, a filial flower, another scent — if I had scoured *the* country, where would the nights and the dreams have strayed? A life slips by, work finishes and begins anew, an estate is mortgaged, crumbles to dust — a war, a love-affair, are born, come to nothing, another war — what's that, another war? Yes, one more. So I ask you, where is one to take one's stand, to find security? Whatever exists through sleep behaves exactly like the estates we frequent and survey in the waking state: 'Not bad at all; but the running water must fail in summer. And then, how to heat in winter a living-room nine yards by eleven! And then it's so inconvenient, that right of way, that path through the vines where our neighbours can walk by us whenever they like. . . .'

I do not have access to the periwinkle lions whenever I wish, nor do I desire it. In excess, I should be bored with my lilac beasts. Down with obsession. But it's to do with a staircase, a building, inhabited in vain for over three years. I had the fortune to add some lions, which themselves revealed to me a second courtyard, in depth, much deeper than the first, I mean than the real one. The lift, which, around 1901, used to stop below the top floor — my own — I repossessed, dealt with, fixed, during a quite severe attack of influenza which kept me feverish and secluded. Should I know better than to be pleased with it? The steel pillar that hoists the cage of the lift is bent. Because of this bend the whole works give a little jump to one side on reaching the last landing. That's the exact moment not to botch — hup, a little jump — getting off on to a narrow platform placed slantingly. Because if you do botch it, that little jump, my word. . . . Well, my word, I can't tell you what would happen since I've never missed it. But I know that I mustn't fail. Thanks to the benevolent presence of the purple lions, which climb simultaneously with my lift, I believe I shall never miss it — except once, a certain time, you can guess which.

However tame, and even insipid, my dreams may be, they

have the power to warm, to colour, to prise open the drowsy, listless flower of sleep. Too tame, they sometimes leave me bad-tempered on waking, irritable as a cat with a broken leg in plaster. And I get fed up with it eventually! And I want my leg! You all seem to find it natural for me to be in this state, that I should be not only 'laden with years and honours', as Laurent Tailhade says, but with pain and disability also. I'm fed up! A miracle, a miracle, by thunder! It's about time! There you are, my best friend, looking at me as if you weren't even worried about me. Upon my word!

'It's just,' he says, 'that I'm not. I trust you.'

With words like that, where does that leave me? I suppress my cries. I don't dare to betray this trust, once again I'm 'very well', I'm 'not at all ill'. Into the first ear held out to the telephone I shall let fall my great imitation of Edouard de La Gandara — don't I still seem to hear him when he used to ring me in the mornings?

'Good morning, dear friend, are you well? Yes, yes, I'm fine, I'm very happy, everything is going on splendidly. A friend is calling to show you the binding I've had done for one of your books, a dark blue and deep pink morocco. It's so marvellous, I never tire of admiring it, what a pleasure to see and touch it! I'm having some fruit sent to you, I only wish it were better. Take good care of yourself for those who love you, including me. . . . I hug you both. . . .'

Without ceasing to extol his life, Edouard de La Gandara left it at around eighty with solemn thanksgiving. He was the brother of the taciturn Antonio de La Gandara who painted Polaire as a young model, the Comtesse de Noailles in blue and silver, her sister, the Princesse de Chimay, in pink, Louise de Mornand crowned with feathers, and many another who, desirous of being painted, had to take sides, to be spirals by Boldini or stiff bamboos by Antonio de La Gandara. I have a bad photograph of him cut out of an illustrated magazine and I keep it, not because he was the well-known painter of his time, but simply because he was handsome. He must have been aware of this, yet he did not condescend to render commonplace, by making likeable, the rather palikere,* grave and haughty character of his entire magnificent person. Edouard, his brother, enamoured of all the arts, chose to be an antiquary. As far as furniture and curios went, he had a bold taste, for it takes a deal of audacity to impose the style of a recent epoch. Edouard de La Gandara's gentleness was afraid of nothing. He was one of the first to adopt the furniture of the Second Empire, the strong colours of their materials, their lasting gilding. . . .

My little writing-desk, with two doors and a flap, which I've moved around with and chipped about for over thirty years, came from him. I acquired this item of furniture, which its owner did not much like, for a nominal sum. 'Eduardo, what's wrong with this little writing-desk?' Eduardo lowered his eyes, hesitated : 'I find it slightly . . . slightly Directoire.' He could not have been more cautious in suspecting a fiancée of being a little . . . a little overripe. . . .

I imitate him badly. I lack the optimistic manner, the suave observance of happiness, which were so natural to him. His last present was an 1860 letter-rack with three compartments, encrusted with mother-of-pearl flowers, to which I've entrusted the care of a small museum of pictures whose disorder is only apparent. At first sight it is difficult to see the connection between a young woman in wide woollen trousers standing on the threshold of a Breton cottage, and a schooner stuck in the calm mirror of a Polynesian ocean before a horizon of flat islands. Nothing can account for a list of the services for Good Friday being clipped to the photograph of another young woman : the latter had too brief acclaim in the literary world: Claude Chauvière. The one a meek stay-at-home, the other a sea-rover, they both died, at a few years' interval, at the same age, Chauvière leaving a few novels and Renée Hamon two accounts of journeys to the Antipodes.

They were worth troubling to preserve; they were wont to say that I helped them, but I believe it was they who helped me. In view of the powerful writer's temperament that destroyed

* Greek: heroic, valorous. (Tr.)

Chauvière's frail organism, the thirst for the Pacific that salted the lips of Renée Hamon, I felt constrained to behave towards them in a manner worthy of them and of myself. 'Save me, madame, pick me up again!' wrote Chauvière to me. 'I've fallen down again!' A little later, Renée Hamon, trembling with inexperience: 'I'll never manage, I'll never manage! I've seen things that are too beautiful, I'll never manage to tell about them!' Can one give the waverer a leg-up without putting one's back to it? I put my back to it, with my whole weight. I smothered Chauvière with sufficient encouragement to bruise her all over. I pointed out to Renée Hamon that a book needs other ink than tears. When their mood changed I felt more lighthearted. 'Oh blessed day, madame,' exclaimed Chauvière, 'I'll have finished my novel in a week! It's made my hand hurt. I am a lion, madame! You can hear me roar a mile off.' Poor little lion, who coughed her last feeble roar one Good Friday. . . . She had wanted to be baptized, and I became her god-mother from July 2nd, 1928. The same day she received her first communion. She received it pale, glowing, almost fainting, so much so that her entire dress shook on her. '*In the chapel of Notre-Dame-sous-Terre, at the Monastère de l'Esvière, at Angers.* . . .' Towards the altar, towards that which is above the altar, she lifted her great eyes, on the point of tears.

Not lured on by me, but roused, spurred on, I found in them my own share of warmth. They would have plenty of time, later, to learn that one gives birth away from the flame, and with calculation.

The greater part of the poetry fell to the less cultured of the two. The little Breton from Auray covets neither literary renown nor the profits its brings — she would like a cutter. She comes from afar, as it is, and would like to return there, for ever. She'd like a cutter, and with the cutter to regain the distant seas, the continents crumbled into islands. The extraordinary thing is that she got them. A long while ago now, she might have been surprised at the bend of a Californian road, asleep in a blanket, her head on her bag, one arm between the spokes of her bicycle, with fifty francs in the pocket of her sailor's trousers — she might have been discovered at table, eating Tahitian pig on a leaf platter. In her feeling for solitude and her fatalism, she might be compared with Ida Pfeiffer, of vagabond memory. But patient, and Swiss as well, Ida Pfeiffer succeeded doubly in her undertakings. She did not possess those qualities, exaggerated in defeat, that ingenuity which led 'the little Hamon', in a Marquesan hut or riding the long swell among the native crew of a schooner — she worked her passage by scrubbing the decks and cooking the rice — to hope that she had at last found her inexhaustible country, unending reasons to exclaim, to weep with admiration, to place at the service of a poetic, a childlike lyricism, a great 'Ah!', a sob, an enveloping gesture. . . .

She described herself quite objectively : 'Tall as a hunting dog, rather low in the buttocks, but nice little breasts.' Add, to this brief and forceful portrait, a shock of crew-cut brown hair, a fine forehead, a proud regular profile. Tidy almost to obsession, the interior of her maisonette at la Trinité-sur-Mer shone, polished like her dream boat, until the day when she exchanged it for clinic and hospital beds.

'If I had any cash, I'd buy a cutter. . . . A sturdy cutter, lying well in the water, with its mainsail, its jib and its brutal boom. . . . A cutter with its cockpit where I could straddle my two legs and grasp the tiller with my two hands. Rough days in the monsoon or in the drizzle of the doldrums, watching the weather-sails and fetching to windward.' Thus the first pages of her book sing of boats and journeys, uniquely loved. If this Breton, devoted to Saint Anne, has received her reward, she sails eternally, cloud-rigged, there up above.

She leaves souvenirs which nearly all come from the other side of the globe, fabrics of bark and fibre, wood carved by knives, murmuring shells spotted like jaguars, photographs, besides those she gave me, where the sea is flat and calm at the edge of a torrent of vegetation. Beneath the dark verdure drowse Gauguin's models. A Maori young man and woman gallop on two horses. Horses and youths are naked, in flowery trappings. This Edenish image forms part of a film made by Renée Hamon in the Antipodes, which constituted one of the variations she tried to execute on the theme : 'If I could buy a cutter. . . .' Her legacy is that of a marine bibliophile; taste and care are rivals therein. But she had concealed from me, as several studies bear witness, that she could have been a painter. The little she left is in sober and scrupulous order, as ready for a voyage as to assume a grave and final immobility. The steadfast spirit had prepared for everything.

Ten

I've spoken about the ordered drawers I shall leave behind, and
the few letters my people will find therein. My best friend hasn't
yet recovered from his surprise when, having brushed aside a silk
scarf, the creased empty envelopes from the last post, a buried
address-book, my thimble, the two pairs of scissors and tapestry-
work mingled in superficial disorder, his search reveals a drawer
within which nothing clinks, dances, or strays. I haven't gone as
far as the drawer containing 'little bits of string no good for
anything' which Robert de Montesquiou claimed to have seen
at one of his female relatives'. But my domestic discipline had
already astonished — what am I saying, offended — Sido in the
old days. 'What cupboards. . . .' she would say. It wasn't a com-
pliment, but something that had to be said. She recognized none
of the personal and harmonious disorder of her own wardrobes,
flowery with dried petals, sprigs of citronella, silvery spiders
which she would shut in for a time so that they might destroy
the clothes moths. I'd run into her in the garden, one hand closed
on its mysterious contents: 'Let me by,' she would say, 'can't
you see I've got a fresh spider. . . .'

My companion, too, is almost offended by my well-ordered
accumulation of papers. He says that it doesn't go with the way
I look. He may be right. But it suits me, it's indispensable to the
need I feel not to be given short notice — you will understand
what notice I mean. To be precise, to be ready, to be in order,
it is all one. Georges Wague used to call me 'What's-the-time?' It
is time to put in an appearance, to be — under the dressing-
gown and woollen pyjamas — dressed, with chemise clean, feet
tidy, the rest also. And above all, no debts. I used to associate
with men for whom a debt was a joy, a victory, a stimulating
pretext for diplomacy, a state of victorious malice, and I could
never get used to it. So no debts, and tidy drawers. After which,

come what may. When one has not been bohemian in one's life-time, why falter at the end in what one most professes?

I am capable of whim only within order, or rather in classification. On the cardboard boxes in which I collect old photographs, it says: *Animals and friends. Beauty-spots and music-halls. Children and houses.*

The children, my own and those of two other women, are together as I had hoped for in their childhood. They are to be seen in the houses that were their ports of call and my own, and when one of them amuses himself still with the photograph drawer, his attention goes straight to the essentials, that is, to the setting.

'Ah, that's the little building that was knocked down to make a garage. . . . What a strange idea, instead of making the garage behind the barn. . . .'

'Why didn't you say so, then?'

He shrugs a shoulder: 'Much good that would have done. . . .'

This one, the oldest, is an oldfashioned child, restrained and discouraged by the polite antagonism that reduced to a minimum the relation between father and son. . . .

'Those hazel trees, all the same. . . . Were they red hazel-nuts?'

'Filberts. . . .'

'Filberts, if you insist, you purist. . . .'

On the photograph the clump of filberts is invisible, since it was behind the small building. But the eyes of these former children — my God, the youngest of them is already over thirty — have a special way of exploring these old pictures and of savouring the past through the walls. A snapshot groups the three offspring of different maternal beds. They weren't very handsome, but the photograph catches them at a moment when they resembled themselves almost tragically, the oldest in his worst imitation of Musset, hair wild, blond and salty, wild-eyed, charming, irresponsible and affected. The second — thirteen years old — enclosed, inward-looking, is a brutal little poet who would have died rather than admit he was unhappy, that he was affectionate, rather than betray the least of his lyricisms. In this sturdy boy the pretty delicate nose, the fine, slightly receding chin, betray the mother's son.

With them is to be seen my daughter, in all the bloom of her seven years, flourishing, impenetrable. She used to walk barefoot on broken seashells and thorns; standing on rocky islets she would cry, 'On board!' and drag some driftwood to the shore, aided by a small Breton playmate over whom she tyrannized. Nothing else is revealed of her, save the nobility, the impatience visible in the photograph, of a seven-year-old body, momentarily immobilized and burning to hurl herself again into the interrupted frenzy.

The boys grew up without becoming over-intimate. One of them used to call me 'My dearest mother', the other addressed me as 'Madame'. Was it perhaps the latter who loved me the best? Since these portraits taken on the wing, on the Breton shore, one's never again seen them half-naked, scored by the porous rock and the salt, one's never again seen them all three together.

Eleven

How strange it is, a life removed from any kind of malice. No more benevolent lying, no more personal abuse. Never again to direct my steps in an unforeseen direction, hardly ever again to choose. . . . I have entered into dependence. 'You wanted someone to take you to the Galerie Charpentier? But you only had to say so! What, you felt like sitting on the *terrasse* of the little *bistrot* to eat oysters? Why didn't you say so? We could have telephoned for a car. . . .'

Impromptu, the pleasure might have had exactly the flavour of oysters on the *terrasse*, its salt, its fresh water, the taste of its glass of rather greenish white wine. . . . It might have had the dusty odour of an antique shop. Impromptu pleasure doesn't bother about a taxi. As it is, I have to account for myself : 'What, you aren't hungry? And why aren't you hungry? I'll go and find something for you. . . .' May I not, without causing too much fuss and bother, lack an appetite?

It could be a good occasion to lament that henceforward I've access only to the liberty of the imprisoned. I shan't do so, for the liberty of the imprisoned is vast and secret, but such an affirmation, if I published it, would gain little credence among the women I care about. They and I have known each other too long. Not that I lose interest in those of them who attributed to me the dangerous gift of persuasion. But I should say nothing to them touching the liberty of the imprisoned. On the contrary, I want to learn from them what they know about the other kind of prisoners, who did not all perish, thank God, before having seen their chains fall away and are now free men, free from everything save their wives. From fear of losing the last of youth a new feminine jealousy, less sexual than its predecessor, attacks noble objects and renders itself ugly thereby. It does not blush to show envy towards the affection that developed among

116

fellow-prisoners in the camps where friendship was the only light, the sole warmth. This friendship, its gleam of tears and joy, its pure and virile bonds, dating from prison, is what more than one woman can hardly tolerate. She knows that a woman can succour without falling in love, but that the man who aids his fellow can hardly avoid becoming his friend. She listens to the tone of the dialogue between the two men, a *tutoiement* injurious, so she believes, to that of love. She takes stock, in her jealous style, and compares: 'It was with that man that he shared, *in there*, the bar of chocolate, the last piece of sugar, the bread. . . . It was with him that he made his miraculous escape. . . . For the sake of this man, who slept by his side, he gave up half his blanket. To me he has given only his life. . . .'

If these pages are published you will read therein, my wicked ungrateful woman, you will read therein, my fellow, that right up to the end jealous white-haired love prolongs the inestimable pain of loving.

The rack decorated with mother of pearl also holds within reach some family portraits, the greater part of whose number are four-footed. Animals who passed through my life and halted there too rarely, animals whose features and expression impose a wave of regret, of posthumous love. . . . I'm not altogether done with talking about animals. I've a lioness here. . . . The glossy postcard merely gives her name: Léa. That's how one treats famous personalities. She is lying beside a man who is talking to her, and on his arm she rests a paw that covers it, a heavy paw, trusting, friendly, palm upwards. One can make out the enormous pads of the fingers, and from these wide fleshy pads the white claws spring like stamens. Those who knew Léa will remember that she accepted her captivity without reproach. But I've no need of their honest testimony. I still know how to read what the face of a wild beast says. The pure gaze that Léa turns towards me tells me enough.

Her portrait lies next to those of animals who were happier, if not more resigned: my last bulldog, despairing at growing old, at growing deaf, at not hearing my voice so clearly, at seeing my features only through a mist. Perhaps she was afraid, seeing me so indistinctly, that I might be in process of dying gradually, and at night, each time I lit the lamp, I would surprise her sitting down, watching, holding me with a stare that blindness rendered bluish.

Thanks to the gifts received from domestic animals, I am finally done with egotism. That is why I call my latest, cat and tomcat, 'my last ones'. I hope to resist the temptation to hear about me the feline language with its hundred inflexions. And as for a bitch, its walks would now be too long for me. I submit to becoming bloated from inactivity as I've no choice, but I prefer my bulldog, with her wrestler's shoulders, to have the regimen that makes for a slender waist, an easy pace, a cool nose and a satisfied stomach. My last one shines in her departed beauty in an enormous glossy photograph, a cinema still taken during the making of *La Vagabonde*. This ephemeral film helped on no star's career. But the bulldog, Souci, if we had so wished, she and I, could have earned me a fortune. She appeared, photogenically black-and-white, ears pricked, wearing her ardent expression, her visible intelligence, tense with eagerness, and the public did not stint its applause. Afterwards she resumed her healthy regular existence, the worship she bore me, her ill-will towards the canine species, the little armchair she shared with the Cat. . . .

It may be that I shan't publish these pages. For this is the first time that I am writing as I please. It's a great novelty in the life and behaviour of a writer to cover pages whose fate is undecided. I've been writing for fifty-three years. For fifty-three years the material worries of life and commitments for fixed dates have regulated my work and my existence. 'I've promised my pub-lisher. . . . It must be ready by November at latest. . . .' Novels, stories, serials, skilful enough treatments of truth and fiction, I've escaped from it all. But now the inability to get about, and the years, make it impossible for me to sin by fabrication any longer, and exclude me from any chance of romantic encounters. Henceforth, I possess only the images which unfold on the screen of my window, only the light of a sky or an eye, a constellation, the marvels enlarged by my magnifying-glass. So it is to the glory of God that I accumulate these sheets, devoid as they are of any deforming agreeable feature, of any dialogue between imaginary characters, of an arbitrary ending that kills, maims, separates. I abdicate from humbug. But they may be neither published nor completed. We shall see. For a start, I do without the interposed typewriter, which used to follow my pen at its own pace. Farewell to its flimsy paper, its pale or muddy inks. Later, if I have need of it, it will be time enough to resort to its honest aid. When I was young I used to fiddle when I was writing and I profited from my ignorance of design, as well as from my literary inexperience, to draw while writing. For instance, if I happened to hit on the word 'murmur' and to grope for the continuation of my phrase, this was the time to affix, under each of its equal sections, a little caterpillar's foot, one of those small sucker-feet which cling so tenaciously to a branch. At one end of the word I would depict the rather equine head of the caterpillar, at the other end the terminal tail, a ravishing appendix often formed of silky strands, like spun glass. Instead of the word murmur I had the caterpillar symbol, much prettier. And I'd dream of Alphonse Allais, who, finding in the country one of those brown, opulent, velvet-haired caterpillars which are the marvels of their species, would exclaim: 'Look, a bear. But Lord, how small it is, how small it is!'

Embellished with insects and butterflies, it seemed to me that my manuscripts did not take things seriously. I miss them. Those that survive are not so good. I'm more attached to the correspondence that I preserve in the same way as the photographs. Writing is a design, often a portrait, nearly always a revelation. That of the poets of the last half-century is entitled to its decorative motifs and I amuse myself with the significant graphisms of Henri de Régnier, Pierre Louÿs, d'Annunzio, Madame de Noailles, curlicued, breaking like waves, coiled like viburnum tendrils. The messages of Robert de Montesquiou are calligraphic labyrinths, as are those of Léo Larguier. Wavy poetic gestures, tall leisurely-apposed letters, skilfully contrived margins — such letters are as enjoyable to leaf through as an album, and how can one forbear to smile when they make me recall that Annunzio mischievously used to call me 'Colettina' and 'my sister in St Francis of Assisi'?

A uniformly pompous grace links together the large recurved arabesques of the poets, inflated, *appliqué*, witnesses to a slow toil where fantasy has become the theme. The politician denies himself this curvilinear licence, this vain but significant ornament, for he lacks the time and his thought is of the crowd. When I look at the incisive writing of Louis Barthou I seem to hear his voice, sharp, a little less nasal than Poincaré's but equally penetrating. The writing of Léon, Louis's brother, makes up for this, indulges in downstrokes and nonchalance because Léon was gay and sensual, and witty too. 'You should know that in 1898 I became a Mohammedan, simply to stop people from bothering me because of my several wives. Don't spread it. And come back soon from Morocco. It isn't true that *la patrie est en Tanger*. (Oh!)'

Philippe Berthelot, Sire of Cats, scrabbles at the paper with little strokes, scratches at Renan's 'stupidity', and signs with the figured imprint of a feline paw. And what a formula of greeting at the foot of one of his notes! 'A little rasp of the tongue, a purring while turning round on the leather of the seat of office. Ph.'

I enjoy this lightheartedness in men who were grave, I'm especially glad that they were pleased to laugh with me. Donnay's pranks appear on letter-cards in little improvised verses:

> O my adorable Colette
> With the violet-coloured eye,
> Every, every, every cat
> Applauds with its four paws
> The most becoming of cravats
> That bedecks their Mistress. . . .
> And the very old tomcat purrs.

'P.S. This isn't a quatrain.'

Gabriel Fauré, at a concert, does a pen-drawing, a very faithful caricature, of the composer Koechlin walking on his beard and sends it to me by *pneumatique*. I find my past enjoyable, illustrated by friends with whom I was frivolous. . . .

I have lost, or given away, a worried letter from Poincaré. He had just been elected to the Presidency and wrote to me that he would be unable to relax at the Elysée because of his much-loved cat: 'What may not happen to him in this great garden? I haven't yet had time to see if the gaps between the railings. . . .' The cat also wrote to me, in fine Italian hand.

The coarse witticism of a refined man: that's Lucien Guitry. A long, limp, agreeable letter, yet marked by vacillation: that's Drieu la Rochelle, after his novel *Blèche*. A small tidy handwriting: 'Dear friend, do you happen to have in your possession a letter of mine, on dark blue paper if I'm not mistaken? Its rapturous tone, if my memory serves me right, worries me in case it might fall into hands less affectionate than your own. Would you mind returning it to me? Your Louis de Robert.' If I'm not mistaken. . . . If my memory serves me right. . . . I recall that I felt offended by so much caution and that, from sheer mischief, I kept the letter on dark blue paper. Less young, I should have shown myself less susceptible to the punctilious, refined and fragile author of the *Roman d'un Malade*.

The solitary example of the fine handwriting of a man at once cultured, audacious and restrained reminds me that Mendès was a man superior to his work and his life. His letter, too, is a fine one: it campaigns on behalf of a colleague. I couldn't say how it came into my hands, this letter not meant for me.

Another letter:

'Dearest Colette, today makes three months that I've been at Beaujon. I was kept here by force and I gave in. The brutal whirlpool of life mixes the good and the bad so powerfully. It was not for an ignoramus like me to resist. The magnificent devotion I've found at this hospital restores my will to live. Doctor Lion-Kinberg is determined to cure me, but. . . . They give me frightful injections into the lung. My little dog, who comes to see me twice a week, despises me because I'm ill. Perhaps he's right. It upsets me very much.'

That is. . . . Guess? No, you'll never guess. It's Polaire, at the point of death.* It's Polaire, unknown, unappreciated, her gentleness, her handwriting that of the defeated who seems asleep under the wind.

I don't want it to perish before I do, this epistolary past. I bloom so readily in its warmth, it saddens me only when I have to transfer from one file to the other the letters of a friend who has left us. We'll keep this photograph of Pierre Louÿs's, I'm going to stick it beneath the dedication of *Poétique* : 'To Madame Colette Willy. Why? Why, to teach her to write!' He has a torn collar, coarse thick hair, curls straightened with water, matted like cassowary feathers, and the photograph is dated : 1896. I was not so indulgent to love-letters. Born of the flame, the greater part have already perished in the flame. A reasoned, reasonable incineration for which I should not find it difficult to give excellent motives. Love cast into letters, piously tied with a gold thread, embalmed in sandalwood, is not free from the risk of obsolescence, as I know only too well. Perhaps two centuries might grant a reprieve? As it is. . . . 'Into the fire, you who've destroyed me!' cries the hero of *Voyage où il vous plaira*, as he burns his books. Myself neither lost nor saved, it's good to burn the bushes that once were flowers, the dried herbs with the familiar perfume. Oh, it wasn't a matter of a grand auto-da-fé. Just a modest burning of the stubble. . . .

I recall a woman I once used to know, one of those whom the women of my generation knew only by her hair, resolutely white at her latter end, belatedly, maliciously edifying. She used to maintain that the preserved love-letter gives no one pleasure, that it can give rise to a thousand irritations, and that, rather than create posthumous difficulties, she had destroyed all her own. . . .

'What, all of them?'

She winked her little old lady's eye, which still shone with the colour of a great sapphire.

'No. I've kept one.'

'It must have been a very beautiful letter?'

---

* The actress who played the part of Claudine in the dramatization of Colette's early novel, *Claudine à Paris*. As a publicity stunt, Willy, Colette's first husband, used to take them about together dressed as schoolgirl twins. (Tr.)

'For me. I know it by heart. Shall I tell it to you?'

She let her gaze, not devoid of majesty, wander over her well-kept gardens, her overflowing kitchen-gardens, her luminous sheets of water, and recited:

'The key will be hanging behind the shutter.'

'What's next?'

'That's all.'

She paused before adding:

'Believe me, it was enough.'

It is rare for a bacchante past her prime to refrain from extolling, and if necessary inventing, her sensual adventures. Yet I seemed to see on the cheeks of this one a surge of vainglorious red. A moment later, and once more she was all slander and malicious smiles and, God forgive me, I was imitating her. . . . But it's a style that hardly suits me, this affectation of frivolity about love. Love, bread and butter of my pen and my life! Whenever I sit down to speak ill of you, to disown or deny you, someone rings and the shock causes me to blink with the corner of an eye, to twitch a shoulder, a souvenir of the day when what I gained from you was taken away, that something that comforts me till the end of life. . . . I offer you my apologies, Love, victorious opponent, and to whatever name your final flowering may bear. . . .

Stirring in the moist air, the bud tells as much of the season and its progress as the flower it cradles. The explosive season is on its way, bringing its beneficent humidity. In the mornings, at dawn, the odour of mist fills my room. 'It's unhealthy,' says Pauline as she shuts the window. But I delight to feel the mucous membranes of my nose as moist as a dog's, not to have a struggle against the ageing dryness of the air.

Those who are healthy, or just young, are full of plans, and the theatres with old pieces brought up to date. Weekly magazines blossom, as numerous as the daisies on one of Dubout's lawns, and the art galleries send invitations to their private views to 'Monsieur Colette'. The stranger who has just telephoned pressed me to take on a lecture tour. . . . A tour! My word, they must think I'm still only fifty. It's a long time since my talks.

I've sent the two little farmers' wives, alone on their reef — paper being scarce everywhere — two great bundles of lined sheets, hieroglyphs rather than manuscripts, spattered with abbreviated words, with signposts in the form of stars, crosses, little snaky indicators like those along the roads. My memory, my eyes, will no longer need to refer to them on any platform. They will do to wrap up a piece of butter, a rabbit, a pair of sausages whenever a pig departs this life. . . . No regrets!

What a life for a woman, the lecture tour, after ordinary touring, and what a dismal task to travel alone — for, if not, what would become of the miserable pittance — to carry, alone, one's suitcase at arm's length, to defy hoarseness and to capture, single-handed, the sympathy of the public. This solitary expense of spirit, when I recall it, has not always taken first place in my more comic adventures. At La Rochelle the obscure alley labelled 'Artistes' Entrance' straddled a black streamlet and led into a glacial hall where, alone, seated at a white wooden table. . . . At Cannes, in hail and ice, I struggled alone against fever, decked with cupping-glasses, sitting on four injections of camphorated oil. At Aix, that same winter, so that I might change my travelling costume for my 'smart' dress, the coffee-room next to the cinema was placed at my disposal. I recapture the clear December, the mistral that threw icy needles and flakes of flint in my eyes. . . . The cold weather in the Midi is no joke.

Don't pity me, there was no occasion for whining, or even for boredom. At La Rochelle I missed the train for fun, because I couldn't tear myself away from a little shop under the arcades which sold — not to be found, even then — magnificent glass marbles, 'taws' stuffed with varicoloured spirals, as beautiful as the 'sulphurs' (I've still got them). In Avignon I rushed through my autograph session, after my 'chat', to hurry to Señor Rafael Paz y Ferrer in his house of marvels, brimming with mother of pearl, twisted glassware, rainbow-dripping chandeliers, pearled embroidery. At Hyères, seriously delayed by the stopping train, it happened that I 'lost' the hall where I was due to speak a few minutes later. I couldn't remember its name, I looked in vain for a poster. I ran as one runs in a nightmare, I couldn't find a car. . . . As you see, none of this is really sad, any more than I was really alone. Is one really alone, in cities and ports?

In what gloomy decrepit theatre was it, at the beginning of an hour of difficult campaigning, that I heard a great cry? Suddenly I saw a lady rise up, standing on an orchestra stall, who tucked up her skirts to her armpits, yapping: 'A mouse! A mouse!' While she was liberally displaying her . . . emotion, a man's voice announced: 'The lecture includes astronomical slides,' and I was not the last to laugh till I cried.

Traversing the centre of France, from La Roche-Guyon to Vichy, from Vichy to Ax-les-Thermes, by car to save time, I was assailed by a heat so ferocious that I took fright and told the driver to stop the car in the shade of a solitary tree. A moment to rush down the slope and I was sitting fully clothed in the little river that flowed down below there. I stayed there for a while, half-immersed, my linen skirt ballooning in the water round me, in a fish-soup of river bleak, crowned with the heavy green-black dragon-flies that haunt the sugary spikes of the meadow-sweet and the umbels of the pink hemp. . . .

At Marseilles, once, I found myself involved in an acrobatic turn, in an immense hall where everything bore the marks of the makeshift. A white wooden step-ladder led me, in full view of everyone, from the orchestra pit to the stage. From the stage a step-ladder reached the heights of a planking established in the flies, so that I might be visible from every point in the hall. Up there tottered a platform, a small table, a desk-lamp from which a flex descended towards the murky eddies below. . . . Hardly had I sat down than the lamp went out. . . . Amid laughter I saw a sort of kinkajou climb up who dealt with the lamp and descended again. He had just got down when the lamp went out again. . . .

The Marseilles public tends to oscillate between two extremes: tender familiarity and ferocity. I felt it swinging from one to the other. Perched over the void and holding the flex which threatened to drag down the lamp, I held out against vertigo. . . . Suddenly Marseilles, so highly strung, lost its temper. Then I had the idea of imposing, if not silence, at least attention. Pointing to the kinkajou mechanic, down below at the end of the wire, I cried : 'Shh! It bites!' And this phrase brought me a great reward of laughter, shouts and Phocacean objurgations whose intent was no longer dubious.

Was all that worth recalling? All the same, I do recall it. Where would I find tales of great deeds? I have never been anything of a pioneer. So leave me to my mice in Caën and my marbles in La Rochelle. I may not always be able to exclude from my painful memoirs and intermittent felicities the posthumous and frenetic life of the divided snake, the wriggling of the headless beetle. But it's quite enough, to enlighten me as to what it is that undoes me as if I were a young woman, it's quite enough — the ring at the door, the start of the shoulder, the quiver of an eyelid.

Twelve

It's Sunday. The garden is empty, empty my house. I've sent off my best friend to whatever pleases him. To what is moist, already turning green, is still bare. My daughter? Somewhere in occupied Germany, where she is collecting material for an impassioned dispatch. Or in a gloomy Parisian lair where she is writing a poem that she won't let me read. Or in her eyrie in Corrèze, planting her garden. She loves her ruin, where the ripe stonework flakes off and which she fills with roses and fruit-trees. She'll come back when she feels like seeing me, her gaze the colour of the shadow under a chestnut-tree and her mouth like a little pot of strawberries, as people used to say. She turns up unexpectedly and I issue some traditional bits of advice : 'Have you got a vest under your coat? Your skirt is too short. Watch out for the traffic. . . .' She laughs. We laugh. Perhaps our laughter, in some indefinable place, disturbs sleeping generations of mothers, who murmur in concert : 'Your skirt is too short. . . . Watch out. . . . Under your coat, have you got . . . ', then subside and go back to sleep, having performed their maternal duty for the moment. Perhaps one, whom I once knew, sighs as she used to sigh in life : 'Ah ! That little one. . . . My God, that little one. . . .' That little one was fifty-five.

The garden is empty. Empty the house, except for me. This almost daily apprenticeship in silence and hermit-like existence is far from unpleasant, and where nowadays could I find reasons for being miserable? This leg. . . . Yes, we know. Enough about this leg. We'll do without that. I am a normal old person, that is, one who is easily amused. Miserable old people are abnormal, sick or wicked. Sometimes they have the excuse of being frightfully oppressed by the generation they have engendered. Which is certainly not my case.

Worse still is the lot of the spruce survivor, stuck with the heavy, over-palatable fruits that he gathered in his prime. He resorts to false aids, little pills, granules, a sadly too-physical culture, the weighing-machine and other beauty products. . . . His motto : 'I shall maintain' is not as good as mine : 'Taciturn but not serious.'

The solitude I cherish today seeks its despondency in the context of my past solitudes, which neither received nor sought support or saviour. Though I was in need of everything, I was unsubmissive to 'whosoever asks shall receive'. I did not ask.

In a confused period of the war, the last war, which disposed of our persons and our possessions, expelling many of us far from our home and work, I received a letter from Edouard Bourdet. With much precaution, circumlocution and subterfuge he tried to make me accept what he possessed in ready cash. I was so close to crying out of friendship that I replied in some such pathetic manner as : 'My God, how stupid you are !' But I had to promise him that, should the occasion arise, I would not seek any other creditor. Since then, still young, kind and handsome, he has been summoned to meet the overwhelming necessity. . . .

I've taken advantage of my solitude to sort out my papers. The rather testamentary nature of such a duty isn't enough to put me off. One of these days I shall attack the photographs, but that will be more for amusement. My photographic museum is so gay ! No one represented therein casts a gloom on it, not even those to whom a somewhat secret memory might be attached. Does one discard the effigy when one has burnt the letter? Yes. . . . No. . . . All the same, one of these days. . . . Tomorrow. . . . And then I weaken, I waver, I shift the author of the burnt letter into the small group of good friends, I incorporate him therein, let's shuffle the mixture well. This is in no way a dismissal. Quite the contrary, the newly-admitted finds a place among the most worthy : Eugène Landoy, who poses with his faithful parrot, the composer Louis de Serres on a little cardboard horse, the procession of the children of Saint-Sauveur entering, for their prizegiving, the *bistrot* which used to place its 'ballroom' at the disposal of the primary schools. . . . A magnificent print: the portraits of M. and Mme Cornet, old employees of my father. The Douanier himself could not have set them better in their little garden in their Sunday best. And who keep them company in the same drawer? Why, La Duse, wearing her signature like a bandolier, poignant, misty and proud — a little malicious nonetheless, it was stronger than she. . . .

And then a young woman, all ringleted, a graceful young woman, ironic, lanky. . . . How I enjoyed the way she used to tell me about the best part of her life: 'I eloped with Maître Chéramy at the end of a dinner-party where I'd met him for the first time. Just as I was, in a moonlight spangled dress. . . . I didn't come back till eleven years later.' Charming, isn't it? (I made use of the episode in the second act of *Chéri*, Mme Peloux *dixit*.) To run away in a cab, perhaps in the rain, the beautiful moonlight dress getting soaked, the frozen young shoulders warmed in the embrace. . . . Perhaps I ought not to have written Maître Chéramy's name in full? Oh, never mind! I can afford to allow myself this small indulgence: to be veracious now and again. The woman was sufficiently beautiful, sufficiently elated, for the lover — I remember he wore large side-whiskers — to tremble with pride, if he hears me in his eternal rest.

I have here, in my disarray where nothing is mislaid, a collection of pretty faces in the style of the day before yesterday. Actresses? Yes, actresses. Famous? Yes. Who's this one? Guess. But you'd never guess. It's only Cléo de Mérode, whom I've never been able to fit into the pattern. She has never changed.

Changed. . . . I finish writing this word and raise my eyes. Was it a magical word? Everything is new. The new, the springtime, arrive as I write. The Palais-Royal stirs at once under the influence of humidity, of light filtered through soft clouds, of warmth. The green mist hanging over the elms is no longer a mist, it is tomorrow's foliage. So soon! Yes, once again it is the sudden season. Let's continue to write; next time I lift my head it may be summer.

If I want some frank enjoyment, I arrange the photographs

bequeathed to me by my dumb career as a mime. In everything to do with the music-hall I encounter a genuine naïvety. Acrobats and dancers, experienced in strength and grace, become wooden in front of the lens. There's not much difference between their portraits and the 'animated' scenes filmed by the late Méliès. I reserve my keenest pleasure for a photograph where my good friend Georges Wague threatens my breast with a knife which is, at the very least, Catalan. I drop my eyes, I half open my mouth for a (silent) cry, but I don't forget, despite the urgency, to bring my left leg forward, knee slightly bent, in the manner of a *diseuse à voix*; Georges Wague, in profile, reveals that he has a gold ring in the lobe of his ear, a false 'rabbit's foot' between ear and cheek, and an unparalleled ferocity of gaze. He's going to stab this proffered breast — this pretty breast. . . . But because the field is so narrow, he has more the air of intending to tattoo his touching victim with the point of the dagger. . . .

And what do you make of this wild girl, shyly ensconced beneath the skin of a newly-killed lion? You might think it rare, in the jungle, for the skin of a newly-killed lion to boast a fringe of cloth festooned with small teeth, and you would be right. But I, I caress with my gaze this dentate cloth, rival of the dancing shoes with Louis XV heels with which are shod, in egalitarian fashion, the Olympian goddesses, the beggar-maids and the ondines, of the music-hall. And then, let's face it, one had to restore, intact, the tawny bedside rug which had been supplied, on loan, by a furrier's.

And this one, and that one! Oh, that beautiful blue one! I'm standing on one foot, Paul Franck supports my waist without having to kneel more than half-way, my other foot steadies me as best it can and the whole forms a strangely polypod grouping. It is apparent from the picture that my role is that of a (very) ragged vagabond, for the hem of my skirt is suitably slashed with scissor-cuts.

And this one, with a knife between my teeth! And this one, dressed as a man, with long trousers! Can I believe my eyes? . . . This one (I shall destroy it, it's too ugly) commemorates a spell at the Théâtre Royal — 6, rue Royale — which, despite its name, held only some sixty seats. I was playing there in a little comedy, *Aux Innocents les Mains pleines*, what's called a really Parisian piece. As Parisian as my Burgundian accent, as the honest author from the Midi who did not sign it, and as the tailor who made up for me a striped maroon lounge-suit, a worthy Belgian named Van Coppenolle. As proof that I'm not lying, I got thirty francs an evening, matinées included, and Yves Mirande played on the same stage in a piece by Yves Mirande, *La Bonne Hôtesse*. Only he acted well. His partner? A short slender beginner, a marvellous comedian, one. . . . Victor Boucher. . . .

I used to listen to them, both of them, behind a set, and I bore them envy because they enjoyed themselves so extravagantly. . . .

The section 'artistic photographs' isn't so bad, either. Draped poses. Aspirations to the Greek. A small pedestal, consisting of an old Bottin concealed under some drapery. Reutlinger would have preferred me to hold a dove perched on my head. I rejected the stuffed pigeon, though it wasn't more ridiculous than the Greek drapery.

And this one? More rags? Yes, more. Rags, an evil spell and blood scattered about gave a satisfactory result, The new materials were aged with the help of acids, if need be I roughened the silk myself with a brick, and rumpling my hair in all directions with both hands before coming on stage, I threaded it with wisps of straw to make believe that I slept in haystacks before setting fire to them. This one here is *Oiseau de nuit*. Rags here, rags there, and a great sweep of rags which I deployed with arms extended behind me like the wings of an owl. In the finale I was nailed against the wall of the farm with jabs of a pitch-fork. . . .

Looking closely at this photograph, survivor of a thousand postcards, I find it rather too cheerful, this fatal Bird. An optimistic owl. . . . It was because, though it didn't show yet, I was carrying a child. It's impressive, the smile of a happy pregnancy.

I remember welcoming the certainty of this late child — I was forty — with a considered mistrust, and keeping quiet about it. It was myself that I mistrusted. It wasn't a matter of physical apprehension. I was worried about my maturity, my possible inaptitude for loving, understanding, absorption. Love — so I thought — had already served me ill in monopolizing me for twenty years in its exclusive servitude.

It is neither beautiful nor good to start a child so hesitantly. Not in the habit of probing my future, for the first time I planned for a definite contingency, when it would have been amply sufficient to think four weeks ahead. I considered, I made myself lucid and reasonable. Intelligent cats usually make bad mothers, sinning through excess of zeal or through distraction. They walk their children, seized by the scruff of the neck; the hollow of an armchair is a comfortable nest, though less so than beneath an eiderdown, but perhaps the peak of comfort resides in the second drawer of the chest of drawers. . . .

The first three months, anxious to act for the best, I divulged my burden to almost no one. Charles Sauerwein gave me his advice as a friend and father of a family. One phrase he used struck me : 'Do you know what you're doing? You're having a man's pregnancy. A pregnancy ought to be more amusing than that. Put your hat on and come and have a strawberry ice at Poirée-Blanche.'

Fortunately, I changed, though I wasn't aware of it at first. Those around me began to comment on my good appearance and good temper. An involuntary smirk was to be seen even on the optimistic owl — for I continued serenely to play in the *Oiseau de Nuit*, with its arranged fights, blows with a pitchfork, the hand-to-hands on the table, under the table. A male pregnancy? A champion's pregnancy, rather. . . . And the flat, muscled belly of a gymnast.

But it happened that, at the fourth month, my friend Georges Wague reminded me of the 'Geneva job'. The Geneva job would come up during the fifth and sixth months. . . . I confessed everything precipitately, leaving behind my two dismayed friends, my two partners, Wague and Christine Kerf, to contemplate the ruins of the Geneva job. . . .

Insidiously, unhurriedly, I was invaded by the beatitude of the woman great with child. I was no longer the prey of any malaise, any unhappiness. Euphoria, purring — what scientific or familiar name can one give to this saving grace? It must certainly have filled me to over-flowing, for I haven't forgotten it and I think of it whenever life no longer brings any satisfaction. . . .

One grows weary of suppressing what one has never said — such as the state of pride, of banal magnificence which I savoured in ripening my fruit. The recollection I have of it is linked with that of the 'Geneva job'. For, after the break-up I inflicted on our act, I called Wague and Christine Kerf back and, strong in my fine health and good humour, I re-established our trio and our plans for separating on a sound basis. Georges Wague, moved, pretended that he wasn't, treated me like a broody wood-owl, and assured me that my child would be day-blind. On the appointed day we departed and I celebrated my new-found importance by choosing the best room at the hotel. The lake cradled the swans on their reflections, the alpine snows were melting wreathed in vapour, I greeted the Swiss bread, the Swiss honey and coffee, with a smile.

'Look out for the cravings,' said Wague. 'What do you have for breakfast, now you're in trouble?'

'The same as before the trouble, *café au lait*.'

'Good, shall I order it for you when I go down, for eight tomorrow morning?'

'At eight o'clock. . . .'

At eight o'clock the next day there was a knock at my door and a hideously affected little voice chirped:

'It's the maid!'

If you have never seen a sturdy lad, all black hair, lean and muscular, half-naked in a chemise borrowed from Kerf, a red ribbon binding his mane to his brow, and done up in a tailored skirt, you can't imagine how much a gay pregnant woman can laugh. Gravely, her banner of black hair — strange adornment for a transvestite! — over her shoulder, Kerf followed, carrying a small tin percolator and preceded by the aroma of fresh coffee.

Good companions! In order that I might have a breakfast that was not like the 'hotel piss', they percolated fresh coffee, boiled the half-litre of milk over an alcohol flame, bought soft rolls every evening, and left the cube of good butter on the window-ledge at night. I was touched, I was pleased, I essayed my thanks; but Wague responded to this gratitude by assuming his chilly Basque expression : 'It's not for you, it's to keep down expenses.' And Kerf added : 'It's not for you, it's for your little one.'

On stage, that night, during the well-managed combat, I felt a precautionary arm insinuate itself between my loins and the table, aiding my exertion which it appeared to paralyse. . . .

Every evening I said a small farewell to one of the good periods of my life. I was well aware that I should regret it. But the cheer-fulness, the purring, the euphoria submerged everything, and I was governed by the calm animality, the unconcern, with which I was charged by my increasing weight and the muffled call of the being I was forming. . . .

Sixth, seventh month. . . . Suitcases to fill, setting off for the Limousin, a lightheartedness that detested rest. . . . As I grew heavier, especially in the evenings, to ascend the road that spiralled round the hill on the way to my dwelling, I had recourse to my two shepherd dogs, Bagheera and Fils; they hauled me along at the ends of their two leashes. The first strawberries, the first roses. . . . Can I call pregnancy anything but a long holiday? One forgets the anguish of the term, one doesn't forget a unique long holiday; I've forgotten none of it. I particularly recall that sleep used to overwhelm me at capricious hours, and that I would be seized, as in my childhood, by the desire to sleep on the ground, on the grass, on warm straw. Unique 'craving', healthy craving. . . .

Towards the end I had the air of a rat that drags a stolen egg. Uncomfortable in myself, I would be too tired to go to bed and would exhaust the resources of a book or a newspaper in a com-fortable armchair before getting into bed. One evening, when I had exhausted a daily paper up to and including the racing fore-casts and the name of the editor, I sank as low as the serial. A high-class serial, all counts and marquises, carriage-horses that knew no other speed, noble beasts, than the triple gallop. . . .

'Feverishly the Count paced up and down his study. His black velvet indoor clothing accentuated even more the pallor of his face. He pressed a bell; a footman appeared.

"Ask Madame the Countess to join me here," ordered the Count sharply.

In a moment Yolande entered. She had lost none of her energy, but it could be seen that she was about to swoon. The Count held out the fatal letter, which quivered in his grasp.

"Madame," he said with teeth clenched, "have you decided to reveal the name of the author of this letter?"

Yolande did not reply directly. Straight and white as a lily, she took a step forward and articulated, heroically:

"Shit on Ernest." '

I re-read the last line to dispel the hallucination. . . . I had read correctly. The revenge of a dismissed typographer? A practical joke? The Countess's reply restored to me the strength to laugh and to get into my bed, on which the June wind, through the French window, scattered acacia flowers.

Even then, the weight and the tiredness did not interrupt my long holiday. I was borne on a shield of privilege and solicitude. 'Take this armchair! — No, it's too low, this one's better. I've made you a strawberry tart — Here's the pattern for the little bootees, you start by casting on fifteen stitches. . . .'

Neither fifteen nor ten. Neither embroidering a bib nor cutting out a vest nor dreaming of snowy wool. When I tried to picture my creature to myself, I imagined her naked and not bedizened. She was satisfied with a sober and practical English layette, without little lace flounces, without fancy patterns, and bought — from superstition — at the last moment.

The 'male pregnancy' did not lose all its rights; I worked on the last part of *L'Entrave*. The child and the novel drove me on, and the *Vie Parisienne*, which was publishing my unfinished novel as a serial, was catching up with me. The child indicated that it was going to arrive first and I screwed on the cap of my fountain-pen.

My long holiday came to an end on a cloudless day in July. The imperious child, on its way towards its second life, ill-treated a body, no less impatient than itself, which resisted. In my small garden, surrounded by gardens, shielded from the sun, furnished with books and magazines, I waited patiently. I heard my neighbour's cocks crowing and the accelerated beating of my heart. When no one was looking, I unhooked the hose from its stand and sprinkled the parched garden — which I should not be able to succour the next day and the days to follow — with some watering on account.

The outcome. . . . The outcome is of no importance, and I do not accord it a place here. The outcome is the prolonged cry that issues from every woman in childbirth. If I want, even today, to hear its echo, I've only to open the window on the Palais-Royal; from under the arcade there rises the modest clamour of a neighbour who is bringing her sixth son into the world. The outcome is sleep and appetite, selfish and restorative. But it's also, once, the attempt to creep towards me of my little swaddled larva which had been put down for a moment on my bed. Animal perfection! She divined, scented, the presence of my forbidden milk, strove towards my stopped-up source. Never have I wept with so rebellious a heart. What is the suffering of asking in vain compared with the pain of denial?

The outcome is the contemplation of a new person who has entered the house without coming in from outside. The outcome, strangely, is the haughty and final rejection by the austere Beauceronne bitch, who never again condescended to enter the nursery. I struggled for a long time to soften the heart of this abstracted enemy, who would brook no rival in my heart, even to offering her my daughter sleeping in my arms, one small hand dangling, with bare rose-coloured feet, even to telling her: 'Look at her, lick her, take her, I give her to you. . . .' The bitch condescended only to an embittered silence, a look of red-gold that soon turned away.

Did I devote enough love to my contemplation? I should not like to say so. True, I had the capacity — I still have — for wonder. I exercised it on that assembly of marvels which is the new-born. Her nails, resembling in their transparency the convex scale of the pink shrimp — the soles of her feet, which have reached us without touching the ground. . . . The light plumage of her lashes, lowered over her cheek, interposed between the scenes of earth and the bluish dream of her eye. . . . The small sex, a barely incised almond, a bivalve precisely closed, lip to lip. . . .

But the meticulous admiration I devoted to my daughter — I did not call it, I did not feel it as love. I waited. I studied the charming authority of my young nurse, who kneaded and powdered the small body with her clenched fists like dough, suspended it by the feet with one hand. I did not derive from these scenes, so long awaited in my life, the vigilance and emulation of besotted mothers. When, then, would be vouchsafed to me the sign that was to mark my second, more difficult, violation? I had to accept that an accumulation of warnings, of furtive, jealous outbursts, of false premonitions — and even of real ones — the pride in managing an existence of which I was the humble creditor, the somewhat perfidious awareness of giving the other love a lesson in modesty, would eventually change me into an ordinary mother. Yet I only regained my equanimity when intelligible speech blossomed on those ravishing lips, when recognition, malice and even tenderness turned a run-of-the-mill baby into a little girl, and a little girl into my daughter.

In the contest between book and childbirth it was the novel, thank God, that came off worse. Honourably, I had returned to the unfinished *L'Entrave*, which did not recover from the blows inflicted by the feeble and triumphant creature. Consider, hypothetical readers, consider the scamped ending, the inadequate corridor through which I desired my diminished heroes to pass. Consider the fine but empty tone of an ending in which they do not believe, and the modal chord, as a musician might say, so hurriedly sounded. . . .

I have, since, tried to rewrite the ending of *L'Entrave*. I have not succeeded. Between the drafting and the resumption I had performed the laborious delectation of procreation. My strain of virility saved me from the danger which threatens the writer, elevated to a happy and tender parent, of becoming a mediocre author, of preferring henceforward the advantages conferred by a visible and material growth : the worship of children, of plants, of breeding in its various forms. Beneath the still young woman that I was, an old boy of forty saw to the wellbeing of a possibly precious part of myself.

If, exceptionally, when I was young I busied myself with some needlework, Sido would shake her divinatory brow : 'You'll never look like anything but a boy sewing.' Had she not said to me : 'You'll never be more than a writer who has produced a child,'? She, at any rate, would not have been unaware of the fortuitous nature of my maternity.

Thirteen

A first flower, pink as a roofing-tile, appears before the leaves at the top of the chestnut-tree before my window. It is an annual exception. On the summit of this tree there is manifest the beginning of spring and the first rust of autumn. It does not fail to flower again, sparsely, in September. I have always found it faithful in its task. Does it think as much of me? For how many hours, how many days, how many years have I been in this place? The time doesn't seem very long; yet the underside of my right sleeve is visibly worn. I need another working jacket, as warm and soft as this one. Maybe it won't need to be very long-wearing. . . . It's curious, this shininess of the right sleeve, which looks as if it had been much licked by moths. The quite trivial to-and-fro of the forearm on the paper shears velvet, polished silk, wears out both wool and myself. We are a one-armed race. One of my mothers-in-law, the second, was practically ambidextrous. She used to sew with her left hand, wrote with her right, painted and dealt cards with the left. She rediscovered Martin's varnish, was the first to hang her walls with 'chocolate paper', anticipated Iribe and Poiret in their essays towards an art of furnishing. Should one conclude from this that ambidexterity indicates a greater imaginativeness in intelligence and performance than we righthanded ones may possess?

The weather's fine. The lawn absorbs the recent rain. The business of the gardener about the flower-beds promises us that, after five years deprived of flowers, we shall once again have the red, pink and violet harmony which distinguishes the Palais-Royal in September. The weather is that of a premature May. I suffer in very bearable fashion, in a rhythm of twinges and waves that I can capitalize musically, as one does the pistons of a train. One of my medical friends has arrived to try out a new and unpublished treatment: injections of a thermal water brought from the source. That's something new, something entertaining. So long as the cure won't have gone out of fashion next summer. . . .

Mme Odehowska's tame nightingale has paid me a visit, with its mistress. It has drunk from my thimble and slept on my shoulder, clothed in the sombre livery, brown streaked with black, of a Polish nightingale. When its beloved mistress summoned it to depart, it betrayed her momentarily by refusing to follow her and whispered something in my ear, then, seeing her go out of the door, uttered a cry and rejoined her. Snug in her corsage, between silk and skin, it went off to take the Métro. One day when it flew off and got lost in the Métro, Pouli had the good sense and composure to stay still on the ground, almost black and very conspicuous against the white stoneware of the wall, waiting, hoping. It saw the arrival of her who sought it, threw itself into her arms. . . . Haven't I anything better to write today? I doubt it. What is it that prevents me from putting a final full-stop here? No part of this miscellany is intended towards a peroration or an apotheosis. 'When will you decide to let us have your memoirs?' Dear publisher, I shan't write them any more, any better, any less than today.

My publishers are all younger than I am. On the evidence of their elders who witnessed my beginnings — their names were Paul Ollendorff, Alfred Vallette, Arthème Fayard, the elder Flammarions, Ferenczi the father and Albin Michel the father-in-law — I believe that their juniors have formed a confused but highly-coloured impression of my life. God forgive them, do they expect a sort of *journal secret*, in the style of the Goncourts? But 'where there is nothing, the king loses his rights'. The publisher too.

It's taken me a long time to scribble some forty volumes. So many hours stolen from travelling, idleness, reading, even from healthy feminine stylishness! How the devil did George Sand manage? That sturdy woman of letters found it possible to finish one novel and start another in the same hour. And she did not thereby lose either a lover or a puff of the narghile, not to mention a *Story of my Life* in twenty volumes, and I am overcome by astonishment. Forcefully, she managed her work, her recoverable sorrows, and her limited pleasures. I couldn't have done as much, and where she thought in terms of the stacked barn, I have lingered to contemplate the green flower of the corn. Mauriac consoles me with the biting praise: 'Where hasn't she foraged, this great bee?'

At the moment she is making a very little honey from the two flowers — they are two now — on the pink chestnut-tree. The day turns towards evening. Is not everything evening, vespers, for me? The days not so much miserly as rapid. Is not the sixth boy who was born this week under my window beginning to walk? The oldest of the six, shepherd of this male flock, leads it to the garden, where it scatters. To get them back again he collects them together, carrying one of his lambs under each arm. They grow like chickens, the one who was crawling begins to run, the one who had his hair done in fat ringlets is cropped like a man, and I get mixed up among them. Everything alters the moment I take my eyes off it. The life of a virtually immobilized being is a vortex of hurry and variety.

What used to make me proud for so long — my competence as a handyman, my acquaintance with hammer and nails, rake and dibber — must be replaced by mere show.

At the age I've reached, didn't Sido wrestle hand-to-hand with the enormous 'Prussian wardrobe', pierced by a bullet in 1870? It's all over for me now, my pride as plumber and cabinet-maker. I pretend to no usefulness other than my existence, and even this utility I confine to those who love me. And having, for half a century, written in black on white, I've written in colours on canvas for the last years.

The blunt needle in my fingers, I guide the wool caught in its oblong eye. My women friends say that I amuse myself thereby, my best friend knows that I find it restful. Simply, I've found my aim therein and have decided that the foliage shall be blue, the marguerite varicoloured, the cherry enormous and marked, at its equator, by four white stitches.

My talent for tapestry-work, as you see, is not recent. This primitive stitchwork, the childhood of the art as it were, I did not dare to make the art of my childhood. The 'boy who sews' thereby unburdens himself of a secret, assumes a satisfying occupation, endorses a virtue nourished by tradition. It was one tactfully adopted by you shadowy young girls of the nineteenth century, stifled in the maternal gloom and drawing the needle. . . . Balzac has an eye on you. 'What are you thinking about, Philomène? You're overstepping the pattern. . . .' Three stitches too many on the tracing of the slipper meant for her father, and Philomène de Watteville will reveal her deep and criminal preoccupation. . . . But she undoes the three stitches that overstep the pattern and begins again, invisibly and perilously, to weave the ruin of Albert Savarus.

The parallelogram of the cross-stitch is so arranged as to give us the illusion of curves. Four stitches outline the round pupil of an eye and sixteen its iris, two hundred constitute a plump strutting dove. A frenzy of ingenuity bewitches the patterns of the cross-stitch. What other art makes use of so many hearts and turtle-doves, forget-me-nots, sheep, umbilicated roses, cushions that say *Papa*, medallions that swear *Friendship*? On a tombstone — is it not so, dear Dignimont — there prays a dog in little squares, while around the mausoleum there flutter cabalistic words such as ABC, DEF, GHIJK, QRSTU. . . . But, leaving on one side the stammerings and the emetic emblems, we find in the best periods of cross-stitch those impetuous flowerings, those colours, which electrify the 'elect'. Either I'm mistaken, or it really seems to me — from the canvas sails, the woollen rigging, the convolvulus flowers which nurse empurpled starfish in their azure funnels — it seems to me that I'm entering harbour.

Some years ago Christian Bérard was attracted by tapestry-work. He was bound to succeed where others had failed, and he filled aristocratic ladies with enthusiasm for the work. These are known not to be the soul of constancy. There remains, I think, of their fine fervour some heavenly blue armchair sewn with ermine tails, some little teneriffe figure with a Sevigné hair-do on a pink background. Then affectation and zeal saw to it that cross-stitch joined macramé and the netting embroidered with darning-stitch in oblivion. To my knowledge, only Mme Lanvin now does tapestry-work because of a desire to do tapestry-work, that is, to project on to canvas the surplus of her raging creative faculties.

It's not for me to say whether my exertions in cross-stitch embroidery are in any way supererogatory. I pierce, I pierce again. The eel of a needle shines between two threads, tows its woollen tail. My memories are written in blue foliage, in pink lilac, in varicoloured marguerites. I shall begin from nature the portrait of my evening star. My thousandfold repeated movement knows all the tunes by heart. 'We scribblers,' Carco used to say, 'we are the only ones who can't sing while we work.' My new work sings. It sings *Boléro* like everyone else. It sings: '*Croyant trouver de la bécasse au bas des prés.* . . .' It sings: '*Quand j'étais chez mon père — Petite camuson.* . . .'

To unlearn how to write, that shouldn't take much time. I can always try. I shall be able to say: 'I'm not concerned with anything here, except this rectangular forget-me-not, this rose shaped like a jam-puff, this silence when the sound of excavation produced by the search for a word has been suppressed.'

Before reaching my goal, I continue to work. I don't know when I shall succeed in not writing; the obsession, the compulsion date back half a century. The little finger of my right hand is somewhat bent because, when writing, the right hand supports itself on it like the kangaroo on its tail. Within me a tired mind continues with its gourmet's search, looks for a better word, and better than better. Fortunately, the idea is less demanding, and well-behaved provided she is well decked out. She is used to waiting, half asleep, for her fresh verbal fodder.

All my life I have taken a good deal of trouble over strangers. Reading me, they fell in love with me and sometimes told me so. Clearly, I can't expect a piece of tapestry-work to win them over in future. . . . How hard it is to set a limit for oneself. . . . If it is necessary only to try, all right, I'll try.

On a resonant road the trotting of two horses harnessed as a pair harmonizes, then falls out of rhythm to harmonize anew. Guided by the same hand, pen and needle, the habit of work and the commonsense desire to bring it to an end become friends, separate, come together again. . . . Try to travel as a team, slow chargers of mine : from here I can see the end of the road.